Rantings
Of
An Old Man

Rantings
Of
An Old Man

Michael Blade

authorHOUSE®

AuthorHouse™ LLC
1663 Liberty Drive
Bloomington, IN 47403
www.authorhouse.com
Phone: 1-800-839-8640

Published by AuthorHouse   04/30/2014

ISBN: 978-1-4969-0691-5 (sc)
ISBN: 978-1-4969-0690-8 (e)

Foreword

This book was written to raise your dander about certain things that you (and everyone else) have to face in this life. I'm talking about the things which many of you get bent out of shape about, yet you forever resist the urge to say anything about those things. And it's not because you are so nice that you hate to complain about anything or anyone; rather, it is because you are so damn afraid to complain about a given matter, because of political correctness, or because you fear being called a bigot, that you find yourself paralyzed when it comes to proclaiming your disdain about what you have seen, heard, experienced, or are experiencing.

Fortunately for you, you have stumbled across someone who doesn't give a rat's ass about political correctness. So, be prepared to be shocked when you read what you are about to read. In that light, you should also be prepared to be confronted with a veritable plethora of swear words which I have used to accentuate certain points that I have attempted to make. It's like a comedian who says a ton of things and nobody laughs—until he uses the word, FUCK—and suddenly everyone is rolling in the aisles with laughter. Of course, I don't care in the least about being funny; what I do care about is making my point/s, and using such words often helps me do that. Hay, I'm old, deal with it.

I could have written a scholarly book like Charles Krauthammer's "Things That Matter," but it takes so much time and effort to be that scholarly, and I just don't have time for that at my age. What's more, I could have refrained from saying what you would call "mean things" about, say, fat people, or homosexuals, or people with those stupid tattoos all over their bodies. But then who wants to read a book about the things some nice old codger has to say? How long would it take you to put that book down? (Unfortunately)

My (other) purpose in writing this book was not, and is not, to hurt the feelings of the people I talk about. After all, I still love people who are fat, or are homosexuals, or have tattoos. I even like Democrats and Republicans along with all the stupid ass socialists who are now trying their best to destroy our country. But, of course, I don't have to like what they do. And you don't either.

Have you ever wanted to write a book about all the things you've seen (and still see) in life that piss you off? Of course you have; but you didn't do it. You're in luck though; I did it for you. And you should thank me for that as practically everyone who reads, "Rantings Of An Old Man," will despise me and call me a bigot, but how awesome that will be for you—because they will not be saying those things about you, let alone to you. So, repeat after me: "Lucky me!"

Intertwined among these articles (rantings) will be a number of short stories that I have written just for this book. They are all original stories and will appear nowhere else (other than in this book). I trust that you will all be able to see my underlying reason for writing each of these articles/rantings and stories. Also, I have included several poems along with a few other tidbits that

I have written just for you. I hope that you will find them to your liking.

Last, I want you to know that I have taught school from Kindergarten through the twelfth grade, and have lectured at a number of Junior Colleges and Colleges during my life on this planet. Those lectures were on a number of subjects including American and World history, politics, and creative writing. I even gave a lecture at a junior college about the female reproduction system as related to birth control pills. You may remain skeptical about all of this, but it is, nevertheless, true. (I can just hear someone eventually saying, "Who would ever let this no-nothing bigot teach in any school, let alone a college?")

You may also be reluctant to believe that both John Kennedy and Ronald Reagan personally asked me to run for a Congressional seat. Delusional, you say? You can think whatever you want. Anyway, there were times when I wish I would have followed their advice. I hope this book prompts you rethink some of the positions you hold on at least some of the matters I have chosen to discuss in this book. One way or another, once you read the words, THE END, I hope that you will find yourself far less prone to live your life satisfied to never voice a negative opinion about at least some of the things that make your life, and the life of many others, miserable.

One last thing. I did something with this book that I would not do in a million years with any other book—I did not have it edited by an independent editor or any editor for that matter. Normally speaking, this would be considered a cardinal sin for a writer who cared about his or her final product. However, I decided early on that I would not let another soul read even one page of this book before it was published. I would simply write it and send it off to my publisher. Why? Because I decided to let no one influence what I had to say, or how I wanted to say it. I apologize, therefore, for the spelling errors you may find, and the improper grammar, inept punctuation, and awkward sentences you will undoubtedly discover. Hopefully, these errors will be worth enduring in favor of the positive benefits you may attain after reading what you are about to read. Were I to be given the choice—I would do the same thing again.

Michael Blade

Table of Rantings

Political Correctness

I'm done with political correctness and all the idiots who play that game. They're not kind loving people just bursting with all of the things that are righteous in this world. They're cowards. Yeah, cowards who are afraid of their own feelings. But even worse, they are afraid to be different from the crowd that says, "This is what you are supposed to think; this is what you are supposed to say. And if you don't you are a crude, rude, bigot, not even worthy to be called a human being."

"Hey, Blade, not all people who value political correctness are what you say they are," a brilliant detractor will say. Really? What a magnificent rebuttal! You know what, do me a favor, go teach college, become a lawyer, become a liberal politician, or a left wing news commentator, the majority of whom are self-righteous bastards who believe they are being as close to perfect as humanly possible. Unfortunately, everyday people are slowly becoming political correctness buffoons as well. Take this test to see if you are a well-trained politically correct parrot:

Choose only one:

1. A homosexual is merely a person who chooses an alternate lifestyle. Morality has nothing to do with it.

2. A homosexual is sick in the head and needs psychological help.
3. A homosexual has the right be so under the law.
4. A homosexual is destined to go to hell.

So, what did you choose? Number one, right? Isn't it wonderful to be politically correct?.

Taking A Walk

I live in a small town which is a suburb of really well known city. It doesn't matter where it is; what I have to say can be said about almost any town or city in this country.

It was around 1 p.m. that afternoon. The rain had just tapered off so the street I was on was relatively clean (if clean means there were no tire shreds, crushed beer cans, rocks, used condoms, and paper bags strewn all over the place). That crap was, however, lined along the curb as far as the eye could see on both sides of that street. Fortunately for me there was a sidewalk. Fortunately also was the fact that I was not blind; had I been I would have tripped on one of the potholes or large cracks in the concrete which were present at intervals of ten feet or less as I walked.

The composition of the street was no different with its own cracks and potholes which were even bigger, wider, and deeper than those on the sidewalk. I marveled at the "superior" maintenance work that had been done some ten years before, and I wondered how the drivers felt as their cars traversed those fat three inch high ropes of tar used to "fix" those old cracks rather than actually repair the damages those maintenance workers were paid to repair. And that is not to mention the new cracks that were there next to the old cracks. As I walked, I remembered a longshoreman named Eric Hoffer whose book I was assigned to read when I was in college way back when. He wasn't exactly an anti-American when compared to the America haters condemning everything that existed in our country back then (as well as today), but there were a lot of things about this country that he didn't like. In his book, "The True Believer," he made it a point to tell the reader that maintenance was the key when it came to determining whether or not a country would continue on, or eventually fold.

In short, you keep on voting for the same morons you have been voting for your whole life, the same people who do nothing but spend your money hoping to buy your votes rather than spend it on fixing our streets, highways, and freeways on which we have to travel, and you will one day discover that Hoffer was absolutely right. Possibly in your lifetime this country will crumble and die, and the lack of adequate maintenance will be one of the main harbingers of that calamity. I hope some of you will eventually catch on to what I (and Hoffer) have told you.

Till then.

Your Main Man, Obama

I don't (didn't) hate President Obama. Fact is, I love his looks, his smile, the way he carries himself, his voice, the words he uses when he talks, the unique things he says when he gives a speech; I like his sense of humor, I like his family, I even like seeing his grey-white hair one week, and his dark-grey hair the following week. Oh yeah, I like the fact that he's interested in sports, that he plays golf and basketball, and that he runs down stairs with his hands bouncing up and down. But most of all I like the fact that because of him this country was finally able to elect a man of color. It was a long time coming, wasn't it?

The things I don't like about him are as follows: he is a fucking socialist, and he's sympathetic with Islam, which means he is sympathetic with radical Islam as well. Let's just say he understands those people. After all, he grew up with them. I also don't appreciate the fact that although he says he is a Christian, he seems as alien to the tenants of Christianity as anyone could ever be. (Notice how quickly he rushes to the aid of Christians every time they are attacked.) What's more, something tells me that he doesn't care too much for Israel. The result of his Muslim upbringing maybe?

There were/are so many brilliant, patriotic black men in this country, yet the public had to choose this "community organizer" and obvious "narcissist" to run the show.

Michael Blade

Obama is a man who will go down in "accurately told history" (if there will ever be such a thing again) as the most inept, most conniving, most deceitful, most wasteful, most divisive President ever elected. He'll make Jimmy Carter look like a mix of both Washington and Lincoln— on steroids! Too bad the history books most people will end up reading will be authored by some of the most deceitful, most slanted historians in existence. Ditto their publishing companies.

I hope this President will be the last one in the history of this country elected solely because of the color of his skin, rather than for his (or her) ability to make our country a better, stronger nation. The same goes for the first woman elected to that post. I'm just afraid that the same mindset will be responsible for electing Hillary, despite the fact that she and her husband will end up fucking up this country even more than Obama did, albeit in a different way. Just remember this, all you liberals, socialists, female power advocates, non-American-Mexicans, black anti-America-Americans, dumb-ass college students, greedy hypocrite union members, and sick-o Wall Street idiots whose goal is to make money no matter what happens in, or to, this country: the Clintons are two of the most deceitful, morally deprived, power-hungry people ever to have "graced" Washington D.C. You sure as hell don't believe that now. But in time many of you will. And those of you who don't believe it are going to deserve everything you get as a result of your stupidity.

You think Obama fucked up this country? Wait 'till Hillary and her behind the scenes "advisor" take over!

Immigration

You can say whatever you want about immigration; the bottom line to EVERYTHING said about it by American politicians—whether right or left—is centered on votes. The Democrats have successfully bought and control the immigrant vote for now, but were the illegal trespassers and legal immigrants currently living in this country to suddenly switch to the Republican Party, every Democrat, every liberal, every socialist, and every union member would be out in the streets picketing to keep "all those foreign bastards out of here!"

It's hilarious to watch the Republicans squirming and wringing their hands over just how to get the Hispanics (and others) living here, legally and illegally, to vote for them. But let's face it-it would take a catastrophic event to turn the minds of the majority of Hispanics living here to vote for a Republican. They know where their bread is buttered. Republicans can be instrumental in passing any pro immigrant bill they want; the Latino population living here (illegally as well as legally) will still reject them every time there is an election. And quit bringing up Reagan. Aliens (many of whom vote illegally), along with a number of Mexican-Americans (et al) might have voted for him, but that was a different era. This is the age of minorities now, and most minority groups are going to shove it to the Republicans no matter what they do or say. And it doesn't matter one bit that the Republicans are right in much of what they say and how they think when it comes to immigration. The majority of the illegal immigrants living here want government handouts, and, rightly, many Republicans don't want to give them the same plethora of government handouts the Democrats literally salivate over giving them just to gain their vote. The ironic thing is if the Republicans were to champion those handouts, trying to buy the minority vote, they would be branded by the leftist press as being dirty conniving hypocrites. And, of course, that would be true, just as it is with the Democrats now.

The Republicans should forgo that hypocrisy; they should stand up and be counted as American patriots, satisfied to go down for the count even if it costs them every future election until our nation finally collapses. And it will fall sooner rather than later if the far left stays in power long enough. What the hell good is it if you are able to say that you are an elected Republican, and then turn around and eat out of the same dog bowl as the politicians on the left who are determined to change (ruin?) this country? Think of it this way: with the influx of millions of Mexicans and other Latinos, Chinese, and Islamic militants, illegally flooding across our borders, it is inevitable that one day the United States will be destroyed—from within. Why? Because when the time comes a huge number of these people will turn against this country. What's more, the majority of blacks—too blind to see that when this country finally does fall, they are going to fall with it—are really going to be shocked when it all goes down. But then it will be too late. I wonder how kind their new rulers are going to be to the blacks and Latinos living here when that time comes—even though a large number of them showed no loyalty to this country as it journeyed toward its demise. And don't for a second think that their new leaders are going to include them (along with their white socialist cohorts) on their list of allies once they establish their new country. History tells us that they will be the first to be eliminated.

And who will these new leaders be? You figure it out. If you can't figure it out now, you will be able to by the time you finish this book.

Maybe Republican conservatives should think about starting a new party during Hillary's reign (if she runs). I just hope that by the time her reign ends both socialism and world (radical) Islam will not have gained an irreversible foothold preventing American patriots from making an effective counter-move. At least those patriots will help give us a few more years of freedom, if they ever do gain power.

Fortunately, there is a remedy to our immigration problem. For the sake of simplicity let's just call it, THE REMEDY.

THE REMEDY:

(I know that what I am about to say will make the left collectively defecate in (its) (their) collective shorts. I just hope that enough people on the left, as well as on the right, will be bright enough to see the value of this potential remedy.)

Let's first agree that immigration is not a bad thing. I mean, what the hell, my father and his family emigrated from Russia in 1905, and my mother's family migrated here from England in the early 1600's. (That's Sixteen Hundreds.) So, I am certainly not anti immigration.

I know this will shock you but I think we should grant *anyone* who wants to come into this country the right to do so as long as they can prove who they are, where they came from, and, verifiably, who, if anyone, has promised them a job here. (My father's family had to do that.) They must also be able to prove that they are not wanted for a crime in their own country. Upon doing this they should be given a temporary visa (good for two years), and a fingerprinted drivers' license-like card with their picture on it. (But not a driver's license, although they would have the right to get that later.) After that they would need to present themselves at an immigration office every four months to prove that they have been following our immigration laws, that there are no warrants out for their arrest, that they are currently working, and that they are having both State and Federal income taxes taken out of their paychecks. If they are not working it should be determined how they are managing to survive without money, and what they are doing to try to find work. The State they are in should help them find work. (I will not elaborate on that.) If they do not comply with these stipulations by the end of the following four month period, they should be sought out, detained, and then deported without haste. If they have committed a crime they should be incarcerated, made to serve their sentence, and then deported with the knowledge that they will be put at the bottom of the list when it comes to re-filing for reentry into this country.

THIS LAW MUST APPLY TO EVERY NON CITIZEN IMMIGRANT CURRENTLY LIVING IN THIS COUNTRY, NO MATTER WHEN THEY CAME HERE, in that every non citizen immigrant currently living here must be compelled to go through the same process a new immigrant must follow. In short, every illegal immigrant/non citizen must comply with this new law no matter when they came here. However, a stipulation could be inserted into the bill preempting anyone who has (provably) lived in this country over a certain number of years (five years?), as long as they apply for citizenship within eighteen months after this law is passed. If they don't they would be subject to deportation.

If the new immigrant follows this procedure to the letter for at least five years, he or she automatically should be allowed to apply for permanent citizenship status, but only if they can prove they have complied with this law for that period of time.

There needs to be three major stipulations in this law which should be put in force the day the law is passed. These stipulations are necessary to make this plan viable:

1) New immigrants WILL NOT BE, MUST NOT BE, entitled to ANY monetary government benefits while existing as a non citizen in this country. In other words NO GOVERNMENT BENEFITS! This includes city, county, state or federal benefits. If an injury or sickness occurs and the immigrant has no funds to pay for medical care, he or she should be entitled to be treated in a hospital emergency room. That will not be considered a government benefit, and the Federal government should pay for it. (That happens now by the way.)

2) If a non-citizen female immigrant has a child while living in this country, that child WILL NOT be automatically given citizenship. However, citizenship will be granted to that child if and when at least one of its legal parents coming here

becomes a legal citizen (by following the tenants of this plan). If one of the child's parents, here legally, dies, and the other parent (if here legally and is identifiable) is absent or unable to carry on the parenting role, the child may stay here with a guardian and may become a legal citizen if it can be shown that he/she has lived here for five consecutive years and is not wanted for a crime committed here. If the children of at least one legal immigrant enters this country with that immigrant, each child's credentials must be presented at the place of entry (birth certificate, etc.), and he/she/they will be eligible for citizenship status after living in this country for a period of five years. (That is to say a fourteen year old coming here with its legal immigrant parent/parents will be eligible to become a citizen at the age of nineteen.) This must all be contingent upon the child being free of a major felony during his or her waiting period.

3) On the day this plan goes into effect, our borders must be closed tighter than the doors of Fort Knox. There are two reasons for this: one) to prevent immigrants from illegally entering our country, and two) to prevent drug traffickers and terrorists from entering our country.

There is only one way to do this efficiently: The Federal Government must place active duty U.S. Armed Services snipers at practical distances along both our northern and southern border, with the standing order to shoot to kill anyone who attempts to enter our country illegally. If we do this it can be guaranteed that the word would quickly spread and illegal border crossings would drop to near zero in a matter of weeks, if not days. In addition, all tunnels should be found and imploded. Tunnel makers and traffickers found in tunnels calculated to be on the U.S. side of the border should be shot on sight. It should be noted that long fences will not be needed along either of our borders except in very obvious strategic places. Example: Duel towns (American/foreign) situated on borders would need high, electrified, fences for logical distances along those borders in addition to the snipers.

Before you collapse at the sheer thought of what you have just read, you need to remember what I said about letting people into this country: Let them in if they can first prove where they are from; have them get licenses, be fingerprinted, and so on. In short, there would be no good reason for an upstanding person to try to sneak across one of our borders when they can enter this country legally. Only criminals, terrorists, and the drug cartel people would opt to sneak across our borders. In other words, the obvious intent of these people would be, in effect, to hurt the citizens of the United States. Hence, we would have the right, indeed, the obligation, to stop them in their tracks by any means at our disposal, including putting a bullet between their ears. We merely would be defending our country against criminals and terrorists.

I would also press for a yearly immigrant quota: say, one or so million people per year. This would be a total number from all countries. This number can be debated by the members of Congress and added to the final bill. Business people and true visitors (vacationers) should not be affected by this bill and would be entitled to a temporary visa which would be attached to their passports.

How could a remedy like this be any simpler? Simple enough, but it will be way over the heads of many of our astute politicians, dominated by the left, who will undoubtedly have mass bouts of anxiety thinking about the three terrorists who might get shot, as I doubt there would be many more than that who would try to sneak across our borders after hearing they are going to get their brains evacuated from their skulls if they attempt to bring their drugs, terrorism, and propensity to commit crimes into our country.

A plan like this would take guts to implement. But you and I both know that it would work. And don't get all flustered because of the violent aspects of this plan. Concentrate on what I've said. Then show this article to our representatives in the House and the Senate. Let them debate the fine points, write the final law (without excluding any of the major points) and send it to the President. That is how you get things done.

As an aside, if a foreigner wishes to work in this country without wanting to become a citizen, a temporary "work only" visa should be made available upon his or her proving the same things an immigrant must be able to prove. A continuing condition of employment (along with proof of taxes having been paid) must be shown by these workers every four months. If this cannot be shown every four months, the foreigner must leave this country, IMMEDIATELY. If they do not do so, a warrant must be issued for his or her arrest. When apprehended the person must be incarcerated for a designated period of time, and then deported. The intricate details of this plan should be worked out by a bipartisan committee of both congressmen and senators.

Each of these two bills should be penned and voted upon without delay, knowing that it would benefit our country along with the immigrants who truly yearn to come here either to work or to become citizens.

The Birther Bullshit

Just thought you might like to know that I have a ton of both African and African-American friends. I mean these people are real Africans and African-Americans, with no need to erroneously use that mantra now used by white liberals and a huge number of black Americans to define themselves. Blacks born here, as were their parents, and their parents, and their parents, should no more be called African-Americans than I should be perpetually called an English-Irish-Russian—German—Canadian-American. A huge portion of these black citizens, now called "African-Americans," can't even find Africa on a large map. Hey, you know what, I'm a stupid fucking white American, born and raised here, and I don't give a damn about where my relatives came from, other than the fact that it might be interesting to study my heritage someday. (By the way, some of my relatives were persecuted when they got here.) But once I do I'm not going to go around demanding that everyone must refer to me as an English—Irish—Russian—German—Canadian-American!

You might be interested to know that a number of my African friends (especially the ones from Kenya) have shown me pictures of a house in Kenya where they emphatically swear Barack Obama was born. They even have pictures of his bedroom. (They also seem to know Obama's relative who lives in America.) They say their relatives back in Kenya used to talk about Obama's birth status with pride until they were told under no uncertain terms to shut the hell up about it because it could spell trouble for the President, of whom they were so proud. And who could blame them: a born and bred Kenyan (in their minds) was now the President of the United States of America! Me—I don't give a damn where he was born at this point. Just like old lady Clinton said: "What difference does it make now!" I mean, what's anyone going to do about it now? Impeach him because he wasn't eligible to be President? Are you kidding? (What's more, maybe these accusations aren't true.) I should add at this point that, strangely, most educated Kenyans don't like Obama now, and I don't give a crap if you don't believe me about that. They say it's because Obama has done nothing to help their country, which they see as being his country. Of course, I don't blame Obama for not wanting to hang out in that part of the world. He wants to separate himself from that scene as much as he can. He's got enough to deal with without having to associate himself with a nation of Africans expecting him to cater to them. Then again, maybe he's just prejudice against them. (That was a pun.)

It will all be over for Obama, eventually. I just hope we can survive the damage he and his cohorts have done to our country in the interim. As they say, "Only time will tell."

Our Judicial System

I hope you are intelligent enough to know that we have about the most fucked up judicial system in existence. It must be changed to a better, more efficient, more honest, more just system. In other words, a complete overhaul of our judicial system must be implemented. It must be changed from a system of ineptly written and administered laws to an identifiable system of JUSTICE. What's more, those operating within this new system should be compelled to follow our Constitution—without exception, in every case.

I have written a treatise on this very subject which includes the revamped justice system alluded to above. But, it's too lengthy to include in this book. Sorry. I think some of you would have found it quite interesting, as well as plausible.

To summarize, we need to establish a revamped system of justice as opposed to the system we currently have which is composed of a mass of conflicting, unintelligible laws, arbitrarily adjudicated by a bunch of inept juries, lawyers, and judges.

One More Thing About Obama

Just thought you'd like to scrutinize the following conglomeration of FACTS about President Obama. As always, I don't give a damn if you don't believe what I say. Truth be told, I would love for one of you to disprove one or more of the following allegations. I would feel much more at ease about him were someone able to do so. However, I don't think you will be able to do so—if your efforts are pursued without bias.

1. Obama is a semi-Christian with Muslim tendencies. If you only knew how much most true-blue Muslims hate Christians (as well as Jews) you would understand why Obama has failed to openly come to the aid of Christians (and Jews) whenever they are attacked. This is not to say that the President hates Christians and Jews; let's just say that he doesn't feel like bending over backwards to defend them.

I don't envy Obama's having to pretend that Islam is foreign to him, because most Muslims (including those believing in his strange brand of Islam) were/are taught at an early age to wish death on any Muslim who switches to, or even mildly professes Christianity, let alone Judaism. So you can bet he's quite cautious when it comes to offending

Muslims, because you'll remember that he supposedly switched to Christianity "long" before he went into politics. He knows most Muslims don't understand where he's coming from and why he did the things he did when it came to switching to Christianity. Bottom line: I think Muslims scare him.

If you show this to a Muslim he will tell you that I am totally full of shit; that I don't understand their religion, and that they wish harm to no one. Really? Read their laws, their Koran, their Hadith. I have, over and over again for many years. Anyway, many Muslims look at Obama as a traitor, but they are wrong about that. In short, he always was, is now, and will be in the future, their friend. You'll see.

2. Obama's wish is to purposely overwhelm the US economy in order to create internal failure, economic disaster, and social chaos thereby destroying capitalism as well as our country from within, creating, as a result, a socialist state with a permanent majority, following not only him but whatever socialist Democrat arises who is willing to follow what he was able to establish during his term as President. Know this: instituting socialized medicine is his main tool to accomplish this goal.

3. More specifically, Obama Care was created to produce two things: 1) a single payer system run by the Federal Government, and 2) a never ending conglomeration of thankful voters devoted to the Democratic Party. What's really disgusting about this is the fact that had the Republicans had the opportunity to do the same sort of thing—they

probably would have done it. Let's face it: we're screwed as a nation!

4. In order to assure this unending imbalance in our voting system, Obama and his cohorts are forever trying to make Puerto Rico a state. This will give him and whoever follows him two new Democrat Senators and five new Democrat Congressmen, along with a mass of new Americans (voters) dependant on the tax payers of this country to support them. Added to that is the fact that Democrats absolutely have to discourage any form of voter I.D. legislation. If every voter is required to show an I.D. before voting, the Democrats would lose thousands of votes (if those votes were honestly checked). I mean, why in hell would the Democratic Party ever want to lose all the illegal votes they get every election! The Republicans could offer to send a limo to every citizen to help him or her register for an I.D. and the Democrats would find a reason to object to it. What a bunch of phony bastards!

Okay, I'm tired of talking about Obama. I'm also tired of the idiots who don't understand and/or don't believe what I'm saying. What am I supposed to do laugh and cheer for myself when the things I (and others) have warned you against come to pass?

Taking A Hike

I don't really like to hike like I did when I was young. But sometimes I do it anyway. Not long ago I drove to a somewhat well known hiking area not far from where I live. The mountain road travels alongside a river. There's a place to stop and park your car alongside that river. From there you can go wherever you want: upriver, downriver, or up into the mountains on the other side of the river. I hadn't been to this area in many years. I expected to see the same beautiful sights I remembered from the past. I was sorely disappointed.

The area was dominated by Latinos, mostly Mexicans (I would guess) who may or may not have been citizens. That's okay. Latinos like to picnic and hike just like everyone else. None of these people were speaking English, but that was okay too; there is no law saying that people who go there have to speak English—especially among their own family members.

There were many families there with little kids all loudly screaming and laughing and running around. It's what my kids did when I took them there. I walked to the edge of the bank overlooking the river and looked down expecting to see the same sights I saw in the past: clear blue water, green trees, thick brush, and rocky shrub covered mountains rising just on the other side of the river.

Gone. All of it. The water was there; it was a murky brown color. As always, the mountains were there, but they were baron now from a multiplicity of fires over the years. There were some trees left but they looked dead. But, it was the brush and the rock-filled sandy shore running along the river that both shocked and disgusted me. There were hundreds of beer cans, and soft drink cans, and tons of garbage strewn about—on the rocks and on the gravely sand banks that followed the river as far as the eye could see in both directions. And on the small trees and brush along the river hung piss-filled, shit-filled diapers, many of which had been there for what seemed a long while. And on the ground beneath them were food-smeared napkins and paper towels and old rotting articles of clothing and single half-buried shoes along with other things that were not even recognizable.

I looked down at this site with disgust. People back when I was young would never have thought of doing this to their mountains and rivers—and that included the Spanish speaking people who went there. I felt sick. Hopefully, the people there on this day would not think of doing such things to their recreational area. But then I watched a family of seven (including a mother and a father) pack to leave, but not before throwing an entire bag of their trash straight into the river! What theee fuck!

"Well, all Latinos don't throw their trash about like that," I can just hear someone proclaim. How wonderfully insightful! I mean, not many people are that insightful—right? And then I saw two other families head for their cars, both leaving behind every bit of their trash. And there were trashcans down there at intervals of fifty feet all along the bank. And when I looked they were almost all empty!

Are all Latinos like that? Of course not. All I can say is that in the old days you never ever saw anything remotely similar to what I saw that day. And like I said, Latinos came there back then. Maybe some of the people coming there now are illegal immigrants who don't give a crap about our country, I thought. I mean, go to some of the countries where they live and you'll see the same thing.

I decided to come back to that very same spot about two months later just to see if anything had changed. The only difference I saw when I got there was the nature of the trash. Some of the old trash was gone, now replaced by newer beer cans and shit-filled diapers, and other pieces of garbage too numerous to enumerate. All I can say is, fuck every Latino (American citizen or not), and every white-trash Gringo asshole, and anyone else who leaves their trash wherever they go, thereby ruining the beauty of the earth that was given to all of us to enjoy.

You know what—double fuck every one of them!

The Old Man

The old man slowly made his way into the bar on 12th Street. It was six in the evening; the bar was empty except for the two bartenders working there. The man took a table near the bar and looked over at the bartenders. Obviously, the bartenders knew who he was because they both shook their heads when they first saw him entering their establishment.

"What'll you have?" Jim, one of the bartenders said with a sigh.

"Whiskey," the old man replied. His voice sounded gruff, but at the same time there was a thread of weariness running through that gruff voice.

"Of course," the other bartender, Bobbie, quietly groaned.

The old man looked down at the table and sighed.

"Heard the paramedics had to save your ass out on the sidewalk the other day," Bobbie said in a loud voice as he began wiping the bar with a damp rag. The two bartenders looked like they were about to laugh, but they resisted.

The old man didn't reply, and the two bartenders didn't see his eyes well as he had turned away from them just in time.

"That's the second time you tried to snuff yourself," wasn't it?" Jim continued with that growling voice people often use to make a sarcastic point.

"Sump-in-lie-cat," the old man quietly replied. Then he gulped down the last of his whiskey. "Gim-me another," he said smacking his glass down on the table.

"Don't piss off the old fuck," Bobbie whispered to his friend. "He's ornery enough as it is."

Jim just shook his head, poured the drink, and walked it to the old man's table. "You going to get drunk again," he said, placing the new glass on the table.

"You got something against people who like to drink," the old man said. Jim just shook his head and walked back behind the bar. The old man straightened out his crooked index finger and began to make circles in the water ringlets made by the bottoms of his two glasses.

"Writing your life story, eh?" Jim smirked.

"Hey, leave his ass alone," Bobbie said. He didn't particularly like the old man, but enough was enough. Besides, he was a paying customer, wasn't he?

"Yeah, I'll let you read it someday," the old man replied. Not even touching his second drink, he slapped a twenty on the table, arose, and without a backward glance he headed for the door.

"Hey, don't you want your change?" Jim shouted. But the old man didn't answer him.

A light rain was falling as the old man made his slightly unstable way along the sidewalk. Sit here for awhile he said to himself as he negotiated his way around the concrete bus bench that was protected by a metal awning above. He hated getting wet. As he sat there looking at the glistening street he replayed the bar scene he had just endured. Why did those two bartenders hate him so much? He had done nothing to them. Then again, a lot of people hated him, he thought. Was it just because he was old?

"Yeah, because I'm old, and I talk back to them; because I refuse to take crap from people anymore," he shouted into the night. He could feel his blood pressure rising. "Are you writing your life's story?" he said, quoting Jim, the bartender. "Yeah, Jim, I am. You want it in a nutshell? Here it is: Married at twenty-five, two kids, a career that paid the bills; son died in Iraq, daughter died in a car crash; wife, unable to cope, left me for another man who had two kids the same ages as our kids were. I got older and older . . . alone . . . always alone. Oh, yeah, I lost my apartment today, Jim. I have a weak to move out and I have nowhere to go. Bottom line: I have nothing, I am nothing, and I have nothing to look forward to—not now, not ever. I'll bet you like that story, right Jim?"

The old man's tears slowly blended with the remnants of rain still dripping down from his naked forehead. His heart ached more and more with each beat. He slowly leaned his head back to rest on the top of the bench. He took a deep breath; he felt dizzy; he closed his eyes, and exhaled. It would be his last breath. He died as he had lived: alone.

Someday I will be that old man. Hell, I am him now.

Voting

I'm so glad I was born in America. Among all of the freedoms we have I think that voting ranks near the top. It used to bother me that a huge percentage of voters have little or no idea why they vote the way they do. I'll not go too deeply into the reasons why this is so. I'll simply make a few observations about this situation, so I can move on to more pleasant subjects. I can't do anything about it anyway.

Both rich and poor people vote their pocketbooks. (Don't come up with the, "Well, not all rich and/or not all poor people vote their pocketbooks," shit for a change, okay?) Anyway, it's a selfish way to vote, but it's understandable. I've always said that America should do what's best for America, and Americans, no matter what or who is involved—including all foreign and all domestic situations. In that light, voting one's pocketbook does make sense. On the other hand, voting one's pocketbook often can be detrimental to our country—to our way of life as well.

Case in point: an out of work man, perfectly capable of working, will tend to vote for a candidate who will extend his welfare goodies hoping that he will never have to work. That hurts the rest of us in a great number of ways. Appropriating money for a strong defense system benefits everyone, but a rich man who votes solely for people who will give him a variety of unfair tax advantages, may benefit, but it may be hurtful to the rest of us because the deficit it causes may deprive us from getting the military weapons we need. In these two cases both the supposed poor man and the rich man are shown to be exceedingly selfish, with each having no regard for the nation as a whole. In short, one who votes his own pocketbook, and says to hell with everyone else, is little more than a selfish jerk. And I hope that offends all of you greedy Wall Street bastards who only care about making money, and couldn't care less about our country.

Reasons to vote for someone or something can be cumulative as well. In other words, there are additional reasons why a person will vote the way he or she does beside his or her pocketbook:

"My family has always voted Republican, and so will I. I don't even have to think about it." If that is why you vote the way you do then please be advised that you are indeed a stupid fuck!

"Democrats are always for the small man." Stupid!

"Republicans care only about the rich." Stupid!

"I'm in a union; I always vote Democrat." Stupid! "Republicans are always more honest than Democrats." Stupid!

"Republicans *always* follow the Constitution." Stupid! "Democrats are more tolerant of people who make mistakes." Stupid!

Listen, it's time you searched for the truth for a change. Then, when you vote, you'll have a righteous reason to believe that your brain is behind the way you vote, instead of your ass. I could go on and on, but you get the picture.

Another huge reason why people vote the way they do is because of their race. Whites are fairly even when

29

it comes to party voting. It's basically always been that way. It's because whites are more or less split along philosophical lines. Blacks vote first and foremost for other blacks, solely because they are black. ("Hey, not all blacks vote exclusively for other blacks . . . ." Yeah, yeah, I know that; we all know that. Keep still for a while, okay?) On the other hand, most blacks will not vote for a black candidate who is a conservative, or a Republican for that matter. This is because they think those black candidates are "Uncle Toms," and not "brothers." In other words black Republican candidates are not really black-black, they just have dark skin and only care about doing the bidding of whitey. I wonder what Lincoln would say about that if he were still alive? The funny thing is most of those "Uncle Toms" have risen above all the bullshit and have made it on their own, just like we all used to be taught to do in school way back when: "You *can* live the American dream . . . we can *all* live the American dream no matter what color we are," we were taught. However, the blacks who don't believe that, and/or who resent those who do, will never accept any philosophy other than the one they now adhere to: "If he ain't a brother, then he ain't no good, and I ain't going to vote for him or her, not ever!" For that very reason the black majority will refuse to vote for someone like Condoleezza Rice who, although black, and a woman, the black majority will always see her as an "Aunt Tomisina." Never mind that she would make an excellent President and would help this nation rise from the mountain of shit into which we have all been plunged.

By the way, what if a white person said, "If he ain't a real white, I ain't going to vote for him (or her)?" It sure seems to me "that mutha-fuckin' crackah," would be called a bigot by most blacks. "Oh, but that's a different story," the entire left would cry. "Yeah, that sort of thing don't count when blacks say it," many blacks would add.

(Saying those things the way I just said them makes me a bigot, right? In other words you can dish it out, but you can't take it.)

And if you're a Mexican, or any other type of Latino, here illegally, you will automatically vote (illegally) for a Democrat. Why? Because you have been told that Democrats are on your side, and that Republicans hate all Mexicans, and that only Democrats will give you things—and on and on. Same story if you're here legally, or a long time citizen, as it will have been drummed into your head that the Democrats will forever take care of you and your family. Think about it all you non-Latinos, if you were a poor American, and you moved to Mexico, and some political party down there promised that its members would perpetually take care of you, who would you vote for—some other political party that told you to go to work and pay your own way? (The truth hurts, doesn't it?)

On the other hand, Americans of Latino descent, whether Mexican or otherwise, who became American citizens long ago, are basically just like any other American citizen. What's more, they're not as easily snowed as the newbies. They know how the system should work, and most of them have made it on their own, and they're proud of themselves for doing so. And they're proud to be Americans as well.

By the way, I'll say it once again: the main reason why Democrat politicians are so fucking hot to give illegal immigrants a so-called (easy) path to citizenship, is because they know the vast majority of those would-be citizens will be beholding to them, and they also know that they (the Democrats) will have the immigrant vote forever.

What's more, if the Republicans openly campaigned for an easy path to citizenship (without the assurance of border protection) they would be doing it because they think the Latinos would suddenly fall in love with them. What a bunch of idiots! Sometimes I think the Republicans are even stupider than the Democrats!

A final reason why people vote the way they do has to do with their religious beliefs, or lack of them. The majority of Christians (except for a large number of black Christians) vote Republican. This is so because Christian ideals are more in line with Republican ideals than with the ideals of the Democratic Party. Democrats will shit their pants upon reading that last statement. I can just see them jumping to their feet, screaming aloud that they are the ones who care about the indigent, the sick, the lame, and the poor; that they are the ones who are following the tenants of Christianity. Oh, really? Is that why the vast majority of them are for murdering the unborn? Is that why they think it's okay to rob the middle class in order to give to those who refuse to work? Let me tell you, the majority of Democrat politicians say all of those sugar coated things for one purpose alone: to chalk up votes. This may be why the Democrats—and the socialist Presidents they back—are satisfied to watch Christians be butchered around the world without lifting a finger to help them? It may be why they are more interested in the murderers (and a host of other types of criminals) getting lenience than they are seeing to it that the ones killed, or hurt because of them, get the justice they deserve. Just remember, Christ was forgiving, but he whipped the hell out of the money changers in the Temple for defiling it. In short, he was just as interested in justice as he was with leniency. Spin that away!

So, no, the Democratic Party does not contain a preponderance of kind hearted Christians, any more than are all Christian Republican Party members worthy of being called model Christians. I'm just saying that Republicans are more in line with Christian thinking and living than is the preponderance of socialists currently controlling the Democratic Party. And if you Catholic Democrats don't believe what I'm saying, then you ought to read a bit of history sometime, as well as the Bible. After all, the Bible has more than 52 weekend Gospel messages in it. You might be surprised what you find if you read that entire book.

The majority of Jews vote for Democrats in this country. It's an anomaly most Republicans can't figure out. Obama is no friend of Israel, not in the least, yet Jews couldn't wait to put their ex on his name when election time came around in both 2008 and 2012. And that was so with most of the democrat Presidents before him. Maybe what you will read next will help you understand this phenomenon:

There are three types of Jews living in this country: Orthodox Jews, Non-orthodox Jews, and non-religious Jews who call themselves Jews, but refrain from associating themselves with both Judaism and the country of Israel.

1. Orthodox Jews: Jews who practice the same rituals, etc. as their forefathers along with their counterparts now living in Israel. The majority of these Jewish/Americans are inclined to vote for Republicans because they know that most Republicans have supported, and will continue to support Israel until the end of time. This, unfortunately, is not a very large group.

2. Non-orthodox Jews: These are Jews who are of Jewish heritage, who practice one phase of Judaism or another, more according to their own whims than anything else. They are sort of like Protestants who pick and choose what they want to believe. When they say they are "non-orthodox" these Jews they are saying, "We are Jews, but we are political/religious Jews who follow some Jewish religious practices, but not others. In other words, like the early Protestants, they are prone to create a certain set of religious rules and tenants (which suit them) and then loosely stick to them. These non-orthodox Jews tend to vote Democrat but only by a slight margin. Then again, it all depends on the issue. They are glad the United States favors Israel, but they are not entirely guided by the fact. A large number of these Jews are guided more by their pocketbooks than by their attachment to Judaism or their devotion to Israel.

3. Non-religious Jews: These Jews may or may not believe in God. They are Jews because of their heritage. In effect they are Jews in name only (JINOs). Jews in this class, who admit to being Jewish, usually do so because of their last names, or because they have some sort of an agenda in which being Jewish will somehow aid them. Most of these people don't give a crap about Israel. The majority of them vote exclusively for Democrats. Many of them are Socialists. Few of these people are poor. Most of them reside in the middle to upper class. Many of the truly rich Jews in this class use their "Jewishness" to aid them monetarily, although that strategy doesn't work as well as it

once did. Many of these Jews can be found in one or another phase of the entertainment business.

To summarize, if one were to add up these three classes of Jews, five eights to three quarters are inclined to vote Democrat. And now you know why. And you also have a better idea why other types of people tend to vote the way they do. But of course you won't agree with what I have said. (Note: People who hate to generalize have a difficult time making a stand on anything.)

Road Rage

The other day I was driving on the freeway trying to find my way to a certain place. I took a wrong turn and had to get back on the freeway going the other way. In the process I unconsciously cut off a guy getting onto the same freeway. I didn't mean to cut him off; we weren't going very fast and no harm was done. But, when I looked in the rearview mirror I saw him giving me the finger. He was screaming at me, but of course I couldn't hear what he was saying. A moment later he raced up and around to my side, then he moved in front of me. At that point he slowed to a crawl and began pumping his breaks. (We were now on the freeway onramp mind you.) When I tried to get around him he cut me off. As close as we now were I could hear him calling me every name in the book.

At this point it appeared as though he was trying to edge me over to the side of the onramp so he could get out of his car and proceed to beat my brains out. I had reached my limit. I stopped my car and stared at him. The cars behind us began to honk. The guy seemed to be getting more pissed by the second. He motioned for me to pull to the far side of the inordinately large ramp we were on. I did. He pulled slightly in front of me and with a loud oath he leaped out of his car and began to circle around its back to the front of my car.

It was then that I calmly reached under my seat and pulled out my 40 caliber semi-automatic pistol, which immediately caused this asshole to come to an abrupt halt when he saw me pointing it directly at his stupid face!

"Okay, okay," he said, waving both his palms in front of his face.

"Get the fuck back into your car, asshole!" I shouted.

"You got it!" he shouted back. And a moment later I waved for him to pull out in front of me, which he did in short order. I followed him onto the freeway whereupon he immediately headed for the fast lane. I stayed in the slow lane and soon turned onto another freeway. Fortunately, I never saw this moron again.

You know, there ought to be some sort of a sign one could make with his hand that would mean, "Gee-whiz, I'm so sorry for cutting you off," or, "for doing whatever I did that I shouldn't have done." Something like making a fist and sticking up your pinky finger. You know, like the sign language sign for the letter "I," standing for, "I'm sorry for doing whatever I did." Make it a universal sign somehow, you know? Anyway, I wonder what that guy would have done had he known that my fierce looking weapon was really a 40 caliber look-alike squirt gun? (I thought it would have ruined the story had I told you that part earlier.)

Bottom line: Think twice before you threaten someone. The gun they may pull on you may shoot real, not water, bullets!

Justice

What the hell's with the notion half the people in this country have that the death penalty should either be abolished or never carried out if one receives that sentence? The really stupid part of that ongoing debate is the fact that many of the people against the death penalty are the very same people who are in love with abortion, which is the outright killing of the unborn (and nowadays even the recently born). What a bunch of hypocrites! A baby in the womb has never intentionally killed anyone; it hasn't even unintentionally killed anyone. Grown people do that. Don't you get that?

Abortion aside, when are we going to start treating criminals like criminals instead of treating them like they are just the products of broken homes, or our broken society, and should, therefore, all be excused for their actions? I'm talking about the criminals who commit murder and maim and hurt people either for the thrill of it, or for revenge, or for monetary gain, among the many other reasons why these people take the live/lives of others. What's more, it is a complete farce to keep these convicted criminals in prison year after year without having the "justice system" act upon the sentence these people earned. Why is this so? It's because we have a fucked up judicial system led by a bunch of idiotic, money-hungry lawyers, liberal judges, and bleeding heart juries. That's why.

The Boston bombers, those two other psycho kids who shot that young Australian man, the Fort Hood shooter, the idiot who kept those girls hostage for ten years, raping them and killing their babies (and the list goes on and on) should all be rotting in their graves by the time this book is published. But, of course, that won't be the case. If none of them commit suicide (the above kidnapper did) they'll be living in their jail cells until they die of old age—at a cost of hundreds of millions of dollars to the American taxpayer. I hate to tell you this, all you (supposedly) soft-hearted hypocrites, their lives are far less important than those who manage to live their lives without killing others.

"The lives of the killers are just as important in the eyes of God as the law abiding citizens in this world," someone is sure to say. My answer to that is—that is very true. The second part of my answer is to add the following: So allow these killers time to repent (if any of them want to repent), then carry out their sentences, and let God deal with them after that. I can assure you He'll know what to do with them. And if some do repent before being put to death, you can rest assured that their lives with God after that will be far more pleasurable than they would be rotting in a prison cell for years on end before they die. Is having them rot in a prison cell a humane sentence? Christians in particular think they are "being Christian" when they declare their opposition to the death penalty. "It's not Christian to take the life of anyone, even a killer," some will say. But I say nonsense! Is it un-Christian to kill someone who is about to kill you?

It is not anti-Christian to put a hardened criminal, especially a violent killer, to death. Nowhere in the Bible does it say that it is. The Bible says, "Thou shall not commit MURDER." It doesn't say, "Thou shall not KILL another human being for any reason. But the anti-death penalty people repeatedly associate the death penalty with the act of murder, denying that there is a difference between the two situations.

But I, and many others, say that the State is not committing murder when it puts a person to death for committing murder. It is taking the life of a person who has unlawfully, and with malice, taken the life of another person. Think about this: When Christ was on the cross, he said nothing about Caesar's right to take the lives of the two criminals at his sides. One of those criminals even said that they both deserve to die for what they had done. And then he asked Christ for forgiveness and begged Him to take him to Paradise; and Christ said that he would do so that very day. What's more, the crucifixion of Christ was the MURDER of Christ, as he had done nothing to warrant the death penalty; indeed, he had murdered no one. Again, read an accredited Bible and you will see that nowhere does it say anything about killing being wrong in every circumstance, but it does say that committing murder is (always) wrong.

The pro death penalty people are not asking the State to wantonly go around killing every criminal in the world. They are asking the State to eliminate the worst of the worst in our society. By the way, I don't remember hearing a whole lot of crying about the Nazi's who were hung after the Nuremberg trials—which means that many anti-death penalty adherents back then, as well as now, were, and still are, hypocrites.

Tell you what: You keep on eliminating the death penalty, no matter what, and the crime rate will continue to rise, just as it has done ever since the vile killers in our society began to realize that their lives are no longer in jeopardy, despite what they have been/are willing to do to other people.

Who Has The Right?

Whether you know it or not, every duly elected leader of every country in this world has the right to maintain his (or her) position AS LONG AS HE FOLLOWS THE LAWS AND THE CONSTITUTION OF HIS COUNTRY AS THEY EXISTED BEFORE HE WAS ELECTED. If, on his own, he changes the laws and Constitution of his country, the people have the inalienable right to either vote or kick that person out of office.

If a leader has not ILLEGIALLY changed the laws and Constitution of his country, and he or she has followed those laws, and some group of people suddenly decides to kick that person out of office instead of voting him out of office in a national election, that group has neither the moral nor legal right to do so, and the army of that nation has the moral obligation to defend that leader at all costs. If the group opposing the leader decides it wants to use violence to accomplish its goals, the Army has every right to use any force necessary to repel and/or destroy that group.

Cases in point: Hosni Mubarak was the legal leader of Egypt. The Muslim Brotherhood wanted him gone because he wasn't Muslim enough. The Army did not stop this revolt although it should have done so because Mubarak was Egypt's legal leader—even though he was a tyrant.

So, Mubarak was overthrown and there was an election. Mohammad Morsi was elected on a democratic platform. During the election democratic laws and a democratic Constitution was constructed. The people of Egypt voted to accept this new president and the new Constitution. But the new president soon began to change those democratic laws that were in place; he also overrode the Constitution of his country. There was a coup and Morsi was overthrown. The army stayed out of it although it accepted the results of the coup because in the Arm's eyes it was a righteous coup, in that the president had been overriding Egypt's Constitution and had been ushering in a series of Muslim laws the majority of the Egyptian people did not want.

Another case in point: Libya's Kadafi was a tyrant. The people wanted him out of office in much the same way that Mubarak was ousted. The army sided against Kadafi, who, unlike Morsi, was never fairly elected. Unfortunately, the Muslim Brotherhood moved in and it now rules the people just as ruthlessly as Kadafi had ruled them.

In these two cases the army more or less stayed out of the way; in effect it let things happen. But in the case of Egypt the Morsi forces wanted /wants to retain that ex-President, even though he tossed out the Egyptian Constitution. Why? Because they are, like Morsi, radical Muslims. The army rightly opposed this. It thus had/ has the right to fight against this force until a new leader, willing to follow and enforce the constitution of that country, is elected. At the same time it is the job of the ex-president's followers to try to make the army look bad. To do this they taunt the army into killing their own (Morsi's) protesters. In short, they force a fight, the army protects itself, and in the process those in opposition to the army are killed. Pictures are taken of the dead "protesters" and the press shows the pictures of these dead bodies all over the world, causing the army to look like nothing but ruthless killers. Of course, pictures of the dead army members are not shown all over the world, making it look like the protesters are the only ones getting killed.

The above scenario has been, and will be, played out all over the world, and don't for a moment think it will not be played in the Free World just as successfully as it has been played elsewhere. In the United States, after Obama is gone and, while in office, Hillary is able to successfully (further) entrench a socialist welfare system, there will be little violence. However, once Hillary is gone (if she is/was elected), and the conservatives finally regain power, a desperate attempt will be made by those conservatives to save our country from its ultimate demise.

This will entail the dismantling of the welfare system that is responsible for bringing this country to its knees. But when this happens, the welfare recipients will rebel and they will try to destroy whoever is in office. The army will be called in to repel the rioters. People will be killed, and it will be Egypt all over again. This time, however, it will be the US Army that will be billed as the bad guys, and the same tactics will be used by the American rebels (and their anti-American allies) as was used in Egypt, and the press here will react just as it did in Egypt. The only difference will be the fact that it is our president and our army whose existence will be challenged.

Just remember, when the time comes these rioters will try to overthrow a President WHO WILL NOT HAVE ILLIMINATED OUR LAWS OR OUR CONSTITUTION. And our army will have every right, indeed, the obligation, to defend our country by any means necessary when it happens.

Bottom line: We have the right to defend our laws, our Constitution, and our loyal citizens by any means necessary. I just hope there will be enough patriots left to do so successfully.

Why So Fat?

When I was growing up we had about three fat people in our school. One had something wrong with her brain, one had something physically wrong with him, and the third person, a girl, was just plain fat; in fact everyone in her family was fat. However, I don't remember anyone ever outwardly making fun of these people. They were simply accepted, and I remember everyone hoping that someday they would find a way to lose weight and "be normal again," even the one with the screwed up brain.

As the years passed more and more people were becoming overweight. Not super fat; just overweight. Even I gained weight after I quit smoking. The thing was if you got a bit overweight you would eventually get pissed about it and you would diet (or whatever) and you would eventually lose weight. In other words you would get back to normal because it was the right thing to do, culturally, and the right thing to do for your body. What's more, you could look in the mirror and feel good about yourself again.

Then, in the early 2000's, people started to get fat by the droves, and they stayed fat! A few years after that everywhere you looked you'd see fucking herds of walruses waddling around, and they'd be acting as though there was nothing noticeably different about the way they looked. Fact is political correctness said that you were not even allowed to notice their weight. And now "big and fat" has become the new "lean and mean." (So the fat people think.)

I say bullshit! Let me tell you fatsos something: that jiggling fat all over your fat ass body looks like shit, and it always will. Just because people who are not fat are forever pretending that they don't see you as a fat ass, it doesn't mean that they are not thinking it to themselves when they see you waddling around. And no, it's not just mean ol' me, and mean ol' people like me who are thinking that; it's practically everyone who does not look like you who are thinking it, though most of them won't admit it. Let's say they are silent because they feel sorry for you and are trying to be kind hearted—or politically correct.

Hey, look, everyone knows that there's something wrong with you, mentally, and I'll bet you know it too—unless you've managed to convince yourself that there is nothing wrong with the way you look. But, of course, you're only fooling yourself; you know that as well, don't you? I also know that is harder than hell for you to lose weight. But you've got to find a way to reverse that bullshit notion in your head that that tells you it is impossible to lose the weight you know you need to lose. (I'm not talking about people with a true medical problem by the way.)

You don't need to lose weight, you still say? Okay, don't. Keep on the way you are and get your stupid diabetes, and your high cholesterol, and high blood pressure, and die early of a heart attack if you want. Piss on your children and the rest of the people who care about you. What the fuck do they know? Besides, you love being fat! Right? Yeah, sure you do.

"Oh, but my husband/wife/boyfriend/girlfriend loves me just the way I am," you will say. Sure they do—if they're fat too! And even if they're not, statistics say that the day will come when they will look at you and they'll wish that they were with someone else. And that day will come, and then you'll be alone. Unless, of course, you are lucky enough to have a mate who wants to keep you fat (and bodily ugly) so they'll never have to worry about someone taking you away from them. That's real true love, ain't it?

By the way, I'm not talking about you and your wife getting heavy when you're old. That's a different story altogether. But even if that condition arises you'd both be better off if you were able to lose weight. After all, you'll have one another for a longer period of time.

Why am I so hung up about fat people? Because I don't like the current politically correct notion that says that I'm supposed to love every disgusting thing I see in this world, because if I don't someone may get their feelings hurt. Then again, people are entitled to look disgusting if that's what they want, but don't ask everyone else to like it.

You may be surprised to know that I weighed over 250 pounds at one time in my life. I now weigh 180 pounds (at six feet one inch) and when I see pictures of myself when I was that fat, I almost barf! I'll admit it—I was a big fat pig back then.

I'll tell you a little story about the reason why I decided to lose weight when I realized I had turned into a fat ass (even though I might not have *looked* that fat at the time):

I was at Disneyland. I was walking from Tomorrowland to Frontierland and as I passed this couple sitting on a bench they began to laugh. It looked like they were laughing at me. I stopped and asked them why they were laughing. (I know it's hard to believe, but I'm not too shy when it comes to such things.) They seemed uncomfortable and obviously didn't want to tell me why they were laughing. I sat on the bench next to them and told them that I would give them a thousand dollars if they would tell me why they were laughing at me. Finally the girl said, "You won't get mad?" I promised them I would not get mad and that I would buy their lunch if they told me. This is what they said:

"We often play this game when we're sitting on a bench in a public place. Okay, the game is we have to hold our breath until we see a thin person walk by, and our faces were turning purple, and just as we were about to pass out a thin girl walked by; she was sort of walking next to you. Anyway, we were glad that we didn't have to die, and we began to laugh, and you heard us."

I thought it was the funniest story I had ever heard. In addition to the thousand they wouldn't accept my offer to buy them lunch, and we finally parted company with smiles and handshakes. But what they said played on me that whole day and into the night, and by the next day I had decided that my days of being a fat ass slob were over. I merely cut my servings in half, used a smaller plate, quit drinking all sodas, drank fat free milk, ate more vegetable and almost no bread—except gluten free/wheat free—and I lost weight like crazy.

Bottom line: Quit fooling yourself, recognize the fact that you look like a blubbery fat ass pig, and lose weight. You'll love yourself for it. (Did you just say, "Fat chance of doing that!")

The Famous

I personally know a ton of famous people. I mean FAMOUS people, including actors, actresses, (most of them now wanting themselves to be known as simply, "actors"), singers, songwriters, political office holders, sports people, and the list goes on. On a scale of one to ten of these people, seven of them consider themselves to be liberal Democrats or Socialists, two consider themselves to be A-political or independent, and one considers himself or herself to be a so called "Tea Party" conservative. (There are probably more conservatives than they are willing to admit in that scale, but that's another story.)

So, why is this scale structured the way it is? There are many reasons for this, but I will list only a few of those reasons because I don't feel like writing an entire treatise on this matter.

1. Movie actors almost always consider themselves to be super sensitive people, way more than the run of the mill person. And actually that is true to a great extent—they are quite sensitive people. Acting is a very tough profession. Besides all of the other reasons I could list, the very act of acting requires one to travel inside his or her character's body and mind to the extent that they become that character. That sort of thing takes a lot out

of a person. In fact, it makes them kind of crazy at times. (At least this is so with a good many actors.) Being the touchy-feely people they are, they tend to identify with people who are needy. Since socialists and liberals reside mainly within the Democratic Party, and since the Democrats have made it their mission to captivate every needy person in order to permanently attain his or her vote, it is a natural for these performers to look to that political party (and their "types") to sympathize with (and for) them in exchange for the perpetual adoration they inevitably receive from them. (Can't you just hear the great ones yelling and screaming, huffing and puffing over what I have just said?) But, hell with them, they know I'm telling the truth.

2. Singers and many other types of performers are only slightly less apt to identify with the liberals and the Democratic Party. I know many of these people would like to openly identify with the Republican Party, especially the conservative Republicans within that Party, but they refrain from doing so out of fear of reprisal from their peers and their audiences, and, of course, the liberal press. So, they keep still about it in favor of their pocketbooks. And you know what—I don't really blame them for it.

I always loved it when an actor or a singer was so freaking big that he (or she) didn't care what anyone thought about his or her being a conservative. They'd just laugh at their detractors and continue on with their career/s. And it pissed the liberals off to no end when they saw the actor's movie (or the singer's record) go viral and make millions, and they couldn't do anything about it. Examples: John Wayne and Clint Eastwood; even Elvis was no flaming liberal (I know, I talked to him about it one day), and there are famous younger actors and singers today in this category. But I won't name those people as I don't want them to get hurt because of what I say. (And you'd be surprised who some of them are.) Anyway, most of these performers flock to the left because they think that is what they are supposed to do. Besides, it's difficult enough trying to make a living as a performer without their cutting their own throats by espousing their conservative values.

3. Here's the biggest reason why so many performers identify with the political left: First and foremost, it is in their monetary interest to do so. Who goes to the movies most? People under the age of twenty-five. Who goes to concerts most? People under the age of twenty-five. Who are these people? High school students (and high school dropouts), and college students. Generally speaking, this huge group has access to money. Even the poor among this group is able to come up with the money it takes to afford the expensive prices the entertainment industry charges. (Don't ask me how they do it.)

From an early age this vast youth-group is nurtured to flock to the Democratic Party; they are molded by their high schools teachers and college professors into believing in big government, anti-Americanism, and the tenants of socialism. And this huge group makes up the bulk of the viewers paying the entertainment industry for its products.

In light of the above, who the hell do you think the performers are going to cater to, conservatives? Yeah, right! And of course at this point certain people on the left who have the balls to read this book will cry out with indignant voices: "Do you really think that none of us have legitimate reasons to believe in the tenants of the Democratic Party, and liberalism, and socialism?" And, "Do you believe that all we care about is money?"

Here is my answer: I believe that some celebrities have their reasons to align themselves with socialism and liberalism and the Democratic Party, and those reasons have little to do with money. Some others have so much money now that they no longer care about whoreing themselves to the public like they did in the beginning of their careers. In other words, what they do now they do because they legitimately believe in the liberal causes with which they align themselves, just like the conservatives mentioned above who did, or do, the same thing.

Let's face it, liberal entertainers have the right to believe whatever they want to believe; they also have the right to express their views without having to suffer for what they say. By that same token, conservative entertainers have that same right, which means that they should not have to suffer for their views by being boycotted by those on the left in that industry. In other words Matt Damon, Barbara Streisand, Bruce Springsteen, and the others, along with entertainers on the right should be recognized for their talents as entertainers, and left free to partake in whatever political activities they may want to indulge in outside of their professions without having to unjustly pay for it. But don't count on anyone allowing conservative entertainers that right. Only the left wing entertainers are entitled to that!

Maybe it's time for people to appreciate entertainers for their talents rather than for their political persuasions. In other words, listen to and look at their entertainment qualities and discard their political utterances as many of them don't know what the hell they are talking about anyway. Last, maybe it's time for those entertainers to concentrate on entertaining instead of spending their time sucking up to their youthful fans for the money it makes them.

Homosexuals ("Gay?")

I have been around homosexuals since grammar school. Since nearly one hundred percent of them resided in the "closet" no one even suspected that they were homosexuals, or "queers," as the open homosexuals were termed back then. Most of these closeted ones seemed a bit strange in terms of the way they talked and acted. They seemed sort of girlish at times, but most of us brushed it off as being weird, but okay. In other words they were accepted, although the vast majority of them were picked last when it came to choosing up sides when playing whatever sport was in season.

Time passed and we moved on to high school, but still the closeted homosexuals remained in the closet. And even though we now knew what "queers" were, the small number of (closeted) homosexuals in our high school guarded their tendencies all four of the years we were together, so no teasing or bullying ever took place. In fact, if even one of these rather effeminate (yet closeted) fellows were harassed by another student because of the way they acted, that student's ass would have been kicked, because as far as almost everyone was concerned we were all one. That surprises you I'm sure.

And then we graduated and we were on our own, and on their own as well were the homosexuals who were now able to be what they always wanted to be: homosexuals, queers, fags, and finally, gays. Speaking of the term," Gay," literally nobody used that term back then. I remember being introduced to the term they used to describe themselves when several of my friends and I decided to crash this party one night. We had no idea whose party it was, but we walked into the house anyway. Once inside, I remembered looking around the room and seeing the strangest looking group of people I had ever seen. I won't go into detail at this point; let's just say that present was every brand of homosexual/lesbian imaginable! Young, old, white, Latin, black, Asian, cross dressers of both sexes, and the list went on.

On the tables in every room were decks of cards containing the most vile sex pictures imaginable, and there were sex magazines and posters everywhere you looked. Of course, it took only three seconds for my friends and me to issue one another the sign that we had been there long enough. We turned to leave and as we were about to make our exit a man in his forties called out from behind us to wait up.

"Hi, I'm Ralphy," he said. "This is my party."

But before anyone of could say, "Who the fuck cares what your name is; we're out of here," the man said, "I'm sorry if you guys were offended, even though you weren't invited to our little gathering here."

Although his statement was probably well intended, and was, in fact, true, one of my friends felt compelled offer his viewpoint on the matter. "Hey, you know what, we ain't fucking queers; it's just as simple as that. And we're getting the fuck out of here, okay?"

And then Ralphy said it: "Oh, we're not queer, honeybunch; we're just a little gay." And then he laughed, as did several of his friends standing near-by.

"Gay?" one of my other friends replied.

"Yes. We're always happy; you know, like gay means happy. So, we're not queer, I mean like, not weird-queer; we're just a bunch of happy homos, you know?"

I don't think anyone said anything else; I just remember everyone turning and walking back to our car in silence. Once inside the car I remember someone shouting, "Those people were all a bunch of fucking lunatics!" Everyone agreed and then we all broke out in individual choruses of, "We're not queer; we're all just a bunch of happy homos!" And, "We're all just a little gay."

Not long after that I began to hear more and more people referring to homosexuals as, "Gay." Soon it became the name by which they all wanted to be known. And today that is what everyone calls them. Of course, I never call them that. They're still homosexuals/lesbians to me. On the other hand, I don't outwardly call them names, and I'd hate to see anyone bullying them. That sort of thing is downright mean. When I do refer to them I simply call them what they are: homosexuals. They don't like that name now. But I don't give a shit what they like, any more than they care what I like.

I know this will shock you, but I think homosexuals are entitled to do and be whatever they want as long as they keep their antics to themselves and don't offend or hurt straight people in the process. In fact, as far as I'm concerned they can conjure up a ceremony and marry one another any time they want, if that is what they want to do—as long as they don't expect me to see it as a legal or legitimate marriage.

I'll tell you something else that may shock you: the majority of the homosexuals I have met, and still fraternize with on occasion, have been (and are) among the funniest, most amusing, and most talented people one could ever hope to meet. On the other hand, being a teacher of both American and World History, I also know full well that homosexuality has been among the main causes of the collapse of almost every great society since the beginning of civilization. Indeed, the homosexual mentality has bred some of the meanest, most conniving, most ruthless, most vile people in the history of our planet. (Read about some of the antics carried on during Rome's "glorious" past.) And those attributes stem from the very fact that certain societies accepted homosexuality as a legitimate lifestyle. Of course, many of you don't, and won't, believe that. In fact, some of you have probably pissed in your pants over how politically incorrect my comments have been regarding this topic. But hey, I can't help it if you can't face reality. Besides, I am not the manager of history.

I went to a very exclusive, very famous nightclub not long ago. While there, as I was watching a very talented group of dancers and singers, I happened to notice two guys standing in front of me. Not so strange—until I also noticed that each guy had his hand down inside the back of the pants of the other guy, obviously fingering one another's . . . well, you get the point.

The reaction of the other people around me seeing this was mixed. From "no big deal," to quiet reactions of utter disgust could be seen. And of course each of these homosexuals was constantly looking back obviously hoping that someone would say something negative about his/their antics. And, as expected, the politically correct people seeing this were afraid to say anything about what these two fucking idiots were doing. What's more, not one straight couple was doing anything remotely similar to an act of sexual foreplay with one another. The straight people there had more class than that. But homosexuals are in a privileged class now, right?

Me? Did I say something to them like maybe, "Hey, you two fucking idiots—go find a dark alley somewhere!" Answer: Hell no; I didn't say a word. I had friends and relatives with me and I didn't want to cause a scene, or a fight, so we simply moved to another section of the audience, as did most of the people that had been standing around them. Incidentally, it was very possible that some of those who moved away might themselves have been homosexuals equally disgusted with those antics. They are not all that way.

I told you this story not intending to make all homosexuals look like monsters. Rather, I told it as a warning to you, and the warning is this: When you grant a state of normalcy to homosexuals, and their activities, you are asking them to openly perform every vile act their brains can imagine just to show you that they can not only freely perform their disgusting sexual acts any time they want, but that they sure as hell will perform them any time they want—in front of you, your spouse, your elderly mother, or your small children, and they know there ain't a fucking thing you can do about it. Equality? Hey, you know what? Not everything is equal in this world, and there is nothing a homosexual and their liberal minded champions can do to change that.

Like it or not, homosexuality will always be secretly loathed by the majority of the citizens in this country, not to mention the citizens of most of the other countries in this world. True, the older less tolerant generations will die out and new generations will evolve that will be even more tolerant of homosexuality than is the case today. And places like Hollywood and San Francisco, New York City and Palm Springs, et al. will become even bigger Meccas for homosexuals than they are today. But look for those places to degenerate in time. The unfortunate thing is non homosexuals living in those cities will suffer in the process.

A word to homosexuals: I know that you know that what I have said is true. I also know that you know that as each year passes you will gain more public sympathy and will be able to get away with more and more of your antics. But in your quest to prove how "normal" you are, you will never be able to prove that there is some sort of homosexual gene in everyone, just waiting for a chance to mature. (You'd like people to believe that more than anything, wouldn't you?) You can snow a huge portion of the American public, but the majority knows that homosexuality is fostered in an individual for a number of reasons, none of which has to do with genetics.

Feeling certain effeminate urges at a young age does not mean that a given youth is destined to become a homosexual. Those urges tend to fade quite quickly, but if one is "caught" in the middle of that mindset by a homosexual promoter, mass confusion may result in the mind of that non homosexual, and an otherwise normal life may be altered forever. Knowing how to seek help at that time will surely help prevent the catastrophic events that this lifestyle almost always fosters in a person's as he (or she) matures.

Unfortunately, this abnormal lifestyle is being both normalized and promoted by the press, by entertainers, by our schools, and by our politicians. As this condition progresses it will be easier for weak minded people to embrace this activity if certain negative conditions arise in their lives that make this activity look like it might alleviate those negative conditions. When this alternative finally

Michael Blade

becomes the norm, our country will be well on the road to its disintegration. And don't for a moment think that the new rulers (who will take over after this country finally falls) will be as tolerant of homosexuality as today's rulers have been, and will be even more so in the near future. You need only look at Russia, and certain Islamic countries to see what I'm talking about when it comes to the harsh measures some of these countries place on homosexuality and its participants.

As an aside, it might be amusing to straight people to see how desperately homosexuals want to liken their "plight" to the one experienced by black people in this country (past and present). I say amusing because the majority of the black people here don't buy that correlation whatsoever. And they are right: homosexual persecution and black persecution is as different as night and day.

One last thing: It is not necessarily a terrible thing to be a homosexual as long as that homosexual does not participate in the sexual activities in which homosexuals are prone to engage. Unfortunately, not too many non-homosexuals will understand that statement. Unfortunately as well, not too many homosexuals will agree with it either.

God loves all people, including homosexuals. What's more, only God is in a position to judge them. In other words, you and I are permanently excused from assigning them to hell even though some people believe that hell is where every homosexual in the world will go. In any case, since this is still a relatively free country, we are certainly within our rights to condemn what homosexuals do.

60

Tattoos

When I was growing up the only people to have an abundance of tattoos were sailors in the U.S. Navy. I lived not far from Long Beach, C.A., where it was common to see Navy people displaying their tattoos on their arms, and it was not uncommon to see them elsewhere on their bodies. Actually, nobody thought much about it; after all, they were Navy men. They were supposed to do that. Besides, they lived on ships and they seldom flashed their arms about in public areas as they more often than not wore long sleeved garments.

Literally no one in our high school had a tattoo. But, being a bunch of ornery little bastards (as we were) it was natural for a group of six of us to head down to the Pike, in Long Beach, just to mess around, and maybe we'd even be the first students in our high school to get a tattoo, or two. Of course, no one was serious about that—at first. Eventually, everyone began daring one another to get a tattoo. Finally, one guy said that he would get one if I got one. I said I would, not thinking he would go through with it. But he did. He had a small pair of cartoon-like lips drawn on his ass, in red ink, with a blue line around them. It looked stupid! Like Olive Oyl had kissed his rear-end.

Pissed, I knew what I had to do. But like I said, I didn't like the looks of the tattoo he got. I headed out the door with the other five behind me. We walked down the street to another tattoo parlor located on the corner of the street we were on. I told the guy inside to do the lips on my ass thing, but I wanted it to look real. He proceeded to close the blinds and lock the front door of his shop. I whipped down my pants and proceeded to endure the most painful fucking feeling I have ever felt! I guess there are certain areas on a person's rear that are quite sensitive. I think this artist aimed for that spot.

When the guy was finished he gave me a mirror and I beheld the most realistic looking pair of pink lips imaginable. I mean it even had cracks in it; it looked like some chick had really kissed my white ass!

Like I said, I was in high school at the time and I still remember my classmates wondering who kept kissing my ass whenever they saw me in the shower during gym. Years later I learned that the tattoo artist who had tattooed the lips on my ass was one of the most famous tattoo artists ever: Bert Grim! Every tattoo artist knows that name. Although he died years ago, he is still recognized as among the most famous artists ever. Some of the most famous actors in Hollywood back then bragged that they sported one of his works. His studio is still where it was when I got my tattoo, but everything around it looks really different. (I was there just last year. And no, I didn't get a tattoo while I was there.)

Many years passed and tattoos were still quite uncommon amongst the general population. Actually, I, along with the rest of the population, thought that guys who got tattoos that you could see were mainly a bunch of freaking morons. When you saw a bunch of tattoos on someone, and then you looked at his face, you more or less knew he was a moron, or a criminal of some sort. Fact is, criminals, after serving time in this or that prison quite often gave themselves a tattoo in the form of a dot on their hand or face; this mark supposedly designated which prison they had been in. It was like a badge of honor.

More years passed and it was not totally uncommon to see an occasional female with a small tattoo on her person (mainly on her ankle in the beginning). Now it seems that half the younger population has become tattoo crazy, including woman. Practically everywhere you go you see these morons with half their bodies covered with ink. By themselves, some of these tattoos look quite colorful, quite artistic. The only thing is these tattoos are located on these peoples' bodies! And they don't come off!

Hey, listen, you'll probably think I'm a hypocrite, but I think these tattoos make these people look like a bunch of lunatic heathens! And you can multiply that times ten when it comes to women. Nobody could ever see my stupid (ass) tattoo; everybody can see all the shit these people now have marring their bodies! The pitiful thing is these people think that the crap they put all over their bodies looks good: "You know, like, awesome, Dude!" And they purposely wear clothing meant to expose their sometimes colorful, sometimes downright ugly markings, markings which make them look like total baboons.

The majority of these people are in their twenties to forties. But wait until they get older, especially the women. The time will come when those sharp colors and lines will begin to fade. And when that happens these people are going to look like a bunch of fucking slobs! I mean, who the hell wants to see some fat ol' fifty to eighty year old woman with saggy tits and a bunch of shrunken blobs of ink plastered all over her fat-ass body? Oh, but they looked so cool when they were young, right?

Mark my words, when this trend ends, and it will end, the clean bodied people (including those younger than you; maybe even your children's children) are going to look at you with utter disdain. Like, whatever made you do that, Mom, or Dad, Grandma or Grandpa?

Yeah, I know, who am I to judge you? Hay, you know what? You have the right to disfigure your body, and I have the right to say you look like shit! You know what I'm sayin'?

(I'll give whoever wants to heed my words a little piece of inside advice: If you want to make a ton of money, create a way to adequately remove a tattoo, quickly and painlessly, and then make it a business and you'll make a fortune, because mark my words—someday the tattoo rage will be over. And the people without all that shit on them are going to look like they're the most "in" people in the world!)

Viet Nam

Maybe you're not old enough to remember Viet Nam and what went on there. Those of you who are old enough have probably forgotten the particulars in terms of the whys, whens, whos, and hows. All the stupid ass hippies now in their sixties, or older, will remember how they protested the war and eventually saw it end. Those who were for the government's antics will say the whole thing was a tragedy, and that they finally became convinced that we should never have gotten into that war in the first place despite the fact that their beloved President (Kennedy) got them into it.

You probably think that I was for the Viet Nam war and opposed to anyone who protested our involvement there. First of all, I am against war of any kind—unless we, as a nation—are either attacked or are going to be attacked. What's more, I was not "for" the Viet Nam war; I was, however, for protecting the South Vietnamese when they were attacked because they were not capable of protecting themselves against the communists, and I didn't want to see a slaughter there. Last, I don't mind someone protesting an action taken by our government as long as they follow the law in the process. Which brings me to what I thought, and still think, about the Viet Nam war:

THE VIET NAM WAR WAS THE MOST STUPIDLY FOUGHT WAR IN THE HISTORY OF

THE UNITED STATES, IF NOT THE HISTORY OF MAN. In fact, I think Linden Johnson and Richard Nixon and everyone in their combined cabinets should have been arrested for treason and then hung, so ill conceived was their methodology when it came to fighting that war! (Yeah, I know, Iraq and Afghanistan was almost as bad.)

I'm not about to go into the entire history of that stupid war. What I will say is that Kennedy, sympathetic with South Viet Nam because of the north's aggression (and because the South Vietnamese were mostly Catholic), thought that it would be a piece of cake to kick the North's ass. Once we were there (boots on the ground as they say) Kennedy in 1960/61, and later Johnson, still thought the war would be over in a matter of months, if not weeks. They were wrong.

The war began to rage and everyone knew the piece of cake had turned into a piece of shit! Yeah, our kicking the North's ass *should have* been a done deal, but the people in power in our country didn't know what the fuck they were doing. Instead of listening to the generals, the White House and those running it began to cower; they began to listen to the anti war people whose plan was to do anything but fight to win the war.

At any given time we could have opted to win that war. At most, it would have taken us four to five weeks to bring the North to its knees, sit them down at the table and dictate the terms of peace to them. Fat chance! As usual we feared what China would do. Just like we did in Korea. And Johnson feared losing the liberal vote.

So, Instead of getting serious about winning the war, we extended it, causing thousands of casualties on each side. Instead of bombing the living shit out of the North, we held back. Instead of going into Cambodia to bomb the crap out of the North Vietnamese' supply lines that flowed like a raging river into the arms of the North Vietnamese soldiers safely camped in the South, Johnson, and later Nixon, forbade our air force to cross those borders. How wonderful! You can go here, but you can't go there. You can bomb this supply line but not that supply line. And when Nixon finally did attempt a number of secret sorties into Cambodia the protesters at home went ape shit. Finally, Nixon did bomb the North, and when the North Vietnamese realized that they were getting bombed out of existence they quickly rushed to the piece table to save their own asses.

But while we were negotiating the unrealistic peace plan we eventually ended up with, the war raged on. And guess what the brilliant idiots in Washington did in the meantime? They began pulling our troops out of the country. And what was their method? They piecemealed out the most experienced soldiers first, instead of taking the troops out brigade by brigade. Oh, how nice! How Fair! The only thing was the newer guys left alone there didn't know what the hell they were doing. The death rate of our soldiers began to markedly increase. Finally, a huge number of our service members began thinking, "Fuck this; I'm not going to get killed for those politicians and asshole generals now safely hiding back in the States." And so it went.

Finally, a peace treaty was signed and the U.S. left Viet Nam, and the North Vietnamese quickly descended on the South, and South Viet Nam fell in a matter of weeks, and thousands of people were slaughtered after we left, in addition to the hundreds of thousands of people slaughtered while we were there—All FOR NOTHING! All because the idiots in Washington thought they could play war and politics at the same time. Could it be that we have done/are doing the same thing today in the Middle East? Nahhhh—couldn't be. And our troops came home, and they were spit upon by the asshole protesters who were not satisfied that they had won the war for themselves and for the North Vietnamese. And we as a nation have suffered the consequences of that war ever since. On the other hand, Jane Fonda is doing well; isn't it fantastic that she got to play Nancy Reagan? Is there a statute of limitations for treason?

Do you think for a moment that this story will ever be told in our high schools and colleges? Of course it won't. And that's too bad because everything I have said is true and can be proven without question.

Bottom line: IF YOU DON'T WANT TO WIN A WAR DON'T JUMP INTO ONE! As alluded to earlier, how long do you think it will take for Iraq and Afghanistan to fall back into the hands of the radical Muslims once Obama and Clinton abandon those countries? After all the blood and treasure we gave up there! How could so many stupid fucking politicians be elected in such a short period of time in our country's history?

He who says history does not repeat itself is a fool!

First Love

Eddie was sixteen. So was Carolyn. They went to the same school, lived a mile away from one another, and they both went to the same church. In the eleventh grade they fell in love—as much as eleventh graders can love one another. They went to all the dances together and every other function requiring a date. Unlike many of their classmates they refrained from having sex. It had to do with church teaching and parental teaching and the trust they had in both.

Eleventh grade ended and still they had not had sex together. The summer came and their families took separate vacations; they did not see much of one another that summer; it was tough on them. Twelfth grade finally began and they were thrilled to be together again. By the middle of the first semester they had overcome their religious and parental principles and were having sex every time they could manage to be alone. It was wonderful! The twentieth time was as wonderful as the first. Well, almost.

Toward the middle of their second semester the two lovebirds began to think about life after graduation. A four year college seemed to be in the cards for Carolyn, and Eddie thought that a junior college would be a good starting point as he wasn't sure about a specific major. But one way or another, marriage certainly would be more than a mere possibility for them. It was more or less a given.

Michael Blade

For Christmas Carolyn gave Eddie a huge teddy bear and Eddie gave Carolyn a silver charm bracelet. By May they had cut their sexual activities down to about two times a week, some weeks only once. They were simply too busy with their school activities. June arrived and they went to the Prom. After the Prom they drove into the mountains and parked in a spot overlooking the city below. It was a beautiful sight. They had sex in the back seat of Eddie's father's car. It was awkward as Eddie struggled to take off his comber bun while Carolyn fought to lift the layers of her formal which ended up covering her eyes as she faced the back window atop Eddie then facing the front window. They laughed moments after reaching a mutual climax. They finally stumbled back into the front seat and forty-five minutes later they were parking Eddie's father's car in front of Carolyn's house; it was 2:30 in the morning.

After several minutes of small talk they bid one another a good night. Eddie meandered down Carolyn's driveway; he pulled off a handful of rose peddles from the rose garden alongside the driveway and began to release them one at a time as he slowly headed toward his car. He paused to look at the starlit sky. His gaze moved to Carolyn's bedroom window; the light was on. A moment later her light went out, and at that moment he had a feeling that he and Carolyn would never have sex again. He wasn't sure why; he just felt it.

On the final day of school Eddie and Carolyn kissed good-bye with the promise that they would go out on the weekend. That was on Tuesday. On Friday Carolyn called Eddie and excitedly told him that she was offered a summer job in Arizona near the college she would be attending in September. Eddie feigned happiness and told her that he would see her on the weekend.

They did go out that weekend. They talked of their possible careers and of their plans to see one another on a regular basis during their college days.

Near the end of the night Carolyn casually told Eddie that she would be leaving for Arizona the following week. Shocked, Eddie looked deeply into Carolyn's eyes. A moment later he jerked his head up. "See you soon." he whispered. They kissed and Eddie drove off into the night. Eddie and Carolyn would never see one another again.

Not long after that Eddie began to think deeply about his and Carolyn's relationship, especially their sexual relationship. Being a believer in the tenants of Christianity, he began to wonder about their sexual relationship. Yeah, it was good and fun and fulfilling. They had said they loved each other a thousand times; it seemingly made what they did okay. Besides, everyone was having sex; it didn't matter what their religion was; it was simply . . . acceptable. After all, they had talked about their eventual marriage; that made it even more acceptable, didn't it?

A few days after Eddie's bout with his own conscience, he learned from one of his new (summer) college classes that the marriage rate for first time sexual partners was less than three percent. It meant that less than three percent of couples having sex for the first time with one another eventually got married. It meant that all their words of love for one another, and all the times they said they were meant for one another, and all the plans they made for their future together, were nothing more than words meant to convince one another to give up their virginity (mainly her virginity), and to keep on having sex after that.

Eddie wondered whether all of it was worth it in light of the fact that Carolyn was probably gone forever, undoubtedly soon to be in the arms of someone else doing the same things they did. And maybe over time she'd even be doing it with a large number of other partners, each time proclaiming their love for one another; each time planning for their eventual marriage, and each time moving on to someone new.

Eddie finally told himself that it was all worth it, and that he was foolish for ever doubting it for one moment. It was the conclusion you would come to, right? After all, that is what you did when you were in high school. And you didn't end up marrying that person, did you? And you and the person you did marry eventually divorced, right? And now you don't even think marriage is a very worthwhile institution, right? Just live together. That's where it's at these days. Right? Say, "Right!"

Maybe you should have stuck to the moral code your parents tried to teach you when you were young. That is, if they actually tried to teach you some sort of moral code. Maybe you should have paid attention to the preacher or priest you had when you used to go to church. Maybe your life would have been better than it turned out to be. Then again, the world has taught you that people who say the things I have just said are full of bull; that they are of another generation, and that your generation is where it's at now.

Right on, Dude; you keep thinking that and together we'll watch this nation crumble. But you don't really care about that, do you? Besides, you'll fit in—no matter what happens in the future. Right?

Intelligence

Not everyone in this world is brilliant. In fact, most of the people in this world are basically ignorant, if not downright stupid. Of course that doesn't mean that most of these people are not good and decent people. Indeed, one does not have to be brilliant to go to heaven, or wherever you think people go after they die—if anywhere. In fact, the majority of the "smart" people will probably go to a place opposite of what one might think of as heaven, mainly because their "superior" intellect often tells them that there is no higher power to begin with, and I don't think the Higher Power likes that too much. As a result, that Higher Power will most likely accommodate those highly intelligent people by sending them off to that other place whereby they may enjoy the fire and brimstone promised them in that book they forever pooh-poohed while here on earth.

That brings me to the topic of cell phones. News Flash: Despite your dumb-ass cell phone, or IPhone, or whatever their calling it now, all those "aps" will never make you smart. All they can do is give you information, or, said more precisely, they can answer many of your random questions. And you can walk around feeling oh so brilliant with all that random information filling your head, but none of it will make you intelligent.

Look, the ignorance that abounds in our population is due to the fact that our public school system is more or less fucked up! At its best it is designed to teach you how to read and write and do basic math—which it doesn't do very well these days. Outside of that it attempts to give you certain facts along with certain methods to help you acquire certain information. At least that's the theory behind it. But its ability to do even those minor tasks is unbelievably lacking. The intelligence rating among the various age levels in our country is shameful. The same is so when matched with the students from a host of other nations. This condition is outright appalling. From first we have moved to nineteenth (or worse by now) in the world in terms of test scores.

Because of the teachers' unions in this country, it is nearly impossible to fire an inept teacher. Indeed, we are stuck with literally thousands of teachers, many of whom may be well meaning, but are, at the same time, turning this country into a nation of baboons! And it's not just the teachers. School administrators are just as much to blame for this condition, as are those empowered to create the curriculum your children are doomed to endure.

Unfortunately, there is a liberal agenda, beginning in kindergarten, continuing throughout grammar school and high school, and utterly permeating most of our colleges. This agenda has turned our once magnificent educational system, and the students it produced, into a nation of current day imbeciles.

Okay, it's time to throw in the "exception thing." Yes, yes, we all know that there are thousands of good teachers in our public schools; we all know that not all college professors are stupid liberals and socialists. We all know that there are tons of brilliant college students and graduates now in the workplace keeping our tattered nation afloat. Okay? Are you happy now? Good; let's hope that keeps you quiet for awhile.

To prove my point all you have to do is walk onto a college campus and pretend you are a pollster. Ask the same questions once asked by a well known pollster:

1. What is the current Vice President's name?
2. Point to Africa on this map. Point to Syria on this map. Point to Iran on this map. You need only choose two of these tasks.
2. Name the three branches of government.
4. Name five American Presidents.
5. Name the first American President.
6. Which political party wanted to end slavery: Republican or Democrat?
7. In what country can be found Arlington cemetery? Great Britton, France, the U.S., Germany?
8. Which came first: The Articles of Confederation or the Magna Carta?
9. Which man was not a U.S. President: Hayes, Polk, Goldwater, Clinton?
10. How many states are in the United States of America?

Zero percent of the college students who were given this test in three different colleges got them all correct. Eighty-five to eighty-nine percent got less than fifty percent correct. The total number polled—six hundred students.

What a fabulous educational system we have! The college students we are producing are stupendous, aren't they? And these same students comprise the majority of the people protesting against whatever they don't like about

America; like they even understand the things they are protesting against. What's worse, a huge number of these students vote in our national elections!

Speaking of protesting, I was in college during the early days of the Viet Nam war. Wherever I went I saw protesters yelling and screaming out their protestations. And many of their stupid signs had misspelled words on them. And the cameras would begin to roll, and the newscasters would do their slanted interviews. And then the cameras would stop and the news people would leave. And instead of the protesters continuing to protest, they would stop, throw down their signs and begin laughing and chattering about how cool it was to be doing what they were doing, that they had been part of "a happening." In other words, it was the thrill of protesting and getting attention rather than the satisfaction of getting their point across to the public, mainly because they didn't have a point to get across; it was the protesting that turned them on. And many of those who did have a point didn't fully understand the ramifications of their protestations.

I once asked a group of protesters what point they were trying to get across.

"That we're anti-war!" one of them shouted.

"Would you have been anti-war when we were fighting Hitler?" I asked.

"No," more than one of them answered.

"Then you're not anti-war," I returned.

"Well, we're against *this* war, and we totally hate Brindin Johnson."

"Brindin?"

"Yeah, that asshole Republican President we have."

"Should we should let the communists take over all of Southeast Asia?"

"We don't care if they take over the whole fucking world as long as they leave us alone," was their unified answer.

"Yeah, as long as we don't have to go to war over it, and maybe get killed," added someone in the group.

I had heard enough from the brilliant college students of Cal State, Los Angeles.

Isn't it odd that the majority of private schools produce the cream of the crop when it comes to the students taking the tests they have to take to get into college? And private school teachers make far less money. Yeah, yeah, I know all the phony arguments against what I just said. Bottom line: The public schools should do what the private schools do: teach what they teach, teach *how* they teach, and adopt the disciplinary rules they have, and our educational system might make a comeback. But first the public must see to it that all the inept teachers can be/are relieved of their positions. Keep the teachers' union if you want, but allow the bad ones to be removed. In addition to their teachers' contributions, "intelligence" is gleaned from the books students read. The thing is, except for math and most science texts, the liberal arts books are so slanted, misleading, and filled with lies and omissions that students inevitably learn to despise almost everything about the United States by the time they graduate. The result: The idiot public is trained to adore socialism and loathe the American way, and they don't even realize it.

Here's a little gem for all you college trained socialists: Socialism has never, can never, and will never work, no matter where it's instituted—unless the country using it has an inexhaustible supply of wealth behind it. (Example: Middle East countries where oil supplies are unending, along with certain small countries in northern Europe that are sent money from all over the world to be hidden in their vaults, there to collect interest for its owners, and by so doing bulge the coffers of those countries in the process. So, yeah, with an inexhaustible supply of money coming in, these countries can afford to spread their wealth around. Of course, nobody talks about the miniscule populations these countries have.

In short, the socialism we are now beginning to "enjoy" will eventually destroy us. And you socialist morons will deserve everything you get when it happens. Thank God I'm old and most likely won't be here to see the destruction of our once great nation!

Oil

I know this is going to astonish you, but guess what: we have as much or more energy resources in our country than anywhere else in the world. Coal, natural gas, and oil lies here in abundance. All we need do is take it out of the ground and use it—use it for the next umpteen years—until new sources of energy are discovered. Add to that wind and solar power and we wouldn't need to kiss the ass of the Middle East, or anyone else, ever again. In other words, we would need to buy our energy no more FOREVER.

I'll warn you now: the day will come when Islam will control almost all of the oil in the world (except our oil). And because we did not act in a manner that would eliminate our having to depend on the Middle East, we are going to end up a second rate nation—even sooner than expected. And that, added to our socialist mentality, will mean our eventual demise.

When the people in Washington tell you that we need to keep our natural resources in reserve (because if we used our own resources it wouldn't be long before we would run out of those resources), you can tell them that they are all a bunch of bald-faced liars; tell them that you know they are being bought off by people in whose interest it is to prevent us from using our own resources. And stop with the global warming bullshit. Yeah, some of the things man is doing is causing a certain amount of warming in our atmosphere, but most warming is the result of natural cycles. What's more, as new forms of energy are discovered, and utilized, the global warming we are now experiencing will be diminished, if not eliminated in terms of its detrimental effects on us. Maybe you scholars ought to spend some time studying earth cycles. You might get a clearer picture of what's really happening to our earth, and why. When enough people do that we will be able to understand how to cope with it.

You want to get rich? Invest in natural gas stocks before the price becomes too costly.

Syria

I'm going to take the next few paragraphs to tell you what we should have done in Syria. Bear with me now.

Before your brilliant President said anything about a stupid "red line," implying that we would "get" Assad and his killers if they used their chemical weapons against his own people, he should have had a concise plan in terms of just how we would strike them, what we should expect immediately after that strike, and how we would handle things after that. But Obama is not only a socialist with an agenda, he is also a supreme bloviater, which means that although he talked tough, he was, at the same time, scared shitless that he would have to do what he said he would do. That is why he pushed everything onto the Congress as he knew damn well that the consensus of that body would be, "Don't do anything," enabling him to get off the proverbial hook.

Obama got lucky once the poison gas confiscation argument got underway. Who knew his buddy, Putin, would rush in to save him? Of course that is/was a sham as well, and that sham eventually will be "discovered" when Syria uses those hidden weapons in the future.

Here is what we should have done:

We should have had the plan I alluded to above ready to be set into motion within two days of a gas attack. If Russia gave us any crap we should have immediately told them to mind their own damn business. We should have added that they (the Russians) were the cause of the attack because Russia was the country that supplied Assad with some of those chemicals in the first place. (That is verifiable.) The rest of their stockpile came from Iraq. Remember the Bush weapons of mass destruction fiasco? Remember the weapons that Iraq supposedly DIDN'T have? You think Iraq might have shipped a few of their weapons to Syria days before the U.N. verification team got there? Ya think? (By the way, that's provable too.)

If Iran had threatened to attack Israel during the Syrian affair, we could have told them to go ahead and do so—that is if they were also prepared to get blown off the face of the earth by not only Israel but the United States as well. And if they freaked out and attacked Israel before making any threats about doing so, it would have given us the right and the obligation to take out every one of their nuclear facilities while we were leveling the rest of that country, because we have stated all along that an attack on Israel would be tantamount to an attack on the United States.

Bottom line: Russia would not have done a thing if we had attacked Assad, and chicken shit Iran would not have risked their nuclear stockpile over an attack by the U.S. on Assad.

But, as usual, it's too late to do any of that now. And our enemies have moved on to a mired of other new and exciting ways they have designed to gain power (like Ukraine). Alas, the left always gets what it wants, and the right is too stupid to know what to do about it. Of course, in the end people always get what they deserve. Is that not so? Syria has now become solidified and Iran and Russia have increased their power in the Middle East. As a result, the U.S. has dropped several notches in terms of its power and prestige in the eyes of the world. Thanks Barack baby. You're agenda is right on schedule.

The Pond

Johnny More was fifty-two. He had a wife, Sherry, and two kids—for awhile. His wife died of breast cancer when Johnny was forty-one. She was thirty-eight. His kids eventually got married; one moved to the opposite coast, the other one moved over a thousand miles away from Johnny. He seldom saw either of them. After all, they had their own lives to live. What's more, their mother was gone, so . . . .

Johnny was forever lonely. He dated a few times, but nobody could measure up to Sherry. He eventually fell back on his gifts. He was a poet, a writer of novels, a jeweler, an artist, an investor, and that wasn't a complete list of his talents.

One cold winter evening Johnny collected a fresh canvas, an easel, and a box of paints and drove down to the public pond located a short distance from his house. He would paint a winter scene. It would be a night scene with the full moon reflecting on the pond; the surrounding tree branches would be barren, and on a bench near the pond's edge would be an old man gazing out across the water, reflecting on the long life he had lived, and the end of that life that he knew could come at any moment. Why else would that old man have been there in the cold, at night, so reasoned Johnny More.

As he neared the pond Johnny caught sight of a figure sitting on the very bench he had in mind to paint. At first he was irritated that someone was there; it was as though his vision of what he expected to see there was now marred. As he neared the bench he was surprised to see the figure of a woman sitting there. When she heard Johnny coming she turned. Johnny was taken aback to see the woman's stunningly beautiful face. "Hi," he said, feeling a bit stupid as he couldn't seem to prevent himself from staring at her.

"Hi," the young girl replied, for indeed Johnny surmised that she could not have been out of her twenties.

"You going to paint a picture?"

"I was thinking about it."

"How exciting! I've never met an artist before; I mean, not a real one."

"Well, I don't know whether I can legitimately be called a *real* artist."

"Have you ever sold a painting?"

"Many times."

"Then you're a real artist."

"Okay, I guess I am."

"What's your name?" the girl said with a smile that made Johnny's heart skip several beats. Or was it that his irregular heart beat had suddenly decided to act up.

"John. John More. I mean it's not like John-John More. It's just John More. Anyway, some people call me Johnny rather than John." The young girl had arisen from the bench and was facing Johnny as he was making a fool of himself. She didn't say a word; she just looked at him with her head slightly cocked to one side.

"So you think I'm crazy now, right?"

"Ah, no, ah, John-John," she said, wrinkling her forehead while feigning a gaze off to her right.

Johnny couldn't help but laugh at the girl's antics. "Okay, so what's your name?" he asked, still laughing.

"Rosy," she answered, although it seemed like her answer was more in the form of a question.

Johnny shook his head. "Naw," he said. "Not Rosy."

"Betty?"

Johnny shook his head again. "You're not a Betty either."

"Rachael?"

Johnny squinted his eyes and squeezed his lips together. "Yeah," he finally said with a slow nod.

Rachael smiled and extended her hand toward Johnny. "You're pretty sharp, Johnny More."

"Comes with age," he said. He marveled how soft her hand was, yet her grip was firm, and Johnny knew he had met a very special young lady.

"So, how old are you, Johnny?"

Johnny thought it was odd that she would ask, but he would be truthful; what could it hurt? "Well, to begin with, I'm older than some of the rocks you can see around here," he said, pointing to the mired of rocks strewn about.

"Come on, you can't be more than . . . than—"

"Ninety."

'No, come on; I'd say you are about, what . . . forty-three?"

"Close," Johnny said.

Rachael waited.

"Fifty-two," Johnny said, lowering head slightly as he spoke.

"Why does that make you feel down? You look a lot younger."

"Because now that you know I'm older than dirt we can never be lovers, or get married, or whatever." With that Johnny More again lowered his head. He hunched over slightly, let his arms dangle at his sides, and topped off his act with a long sigh.

"Oh, my, oh my, you are freaking hilarious Johnny More!" Rachael virtually shouted. "But wait," she began a moment later, "how old do you think I am? I mean, not that it matters or anything."

"Mmmmm—twenty-three, I'd say."

"Ha! I'm thirty-five!" Rachael said. Johnny marveled at her sparkling eyes as she spoke.

"Well you sure as hell don't look it," little girl named Rachael.

There was a pause in their conversation as Johnny began to set up his easel.

"So, can I watch you paint?"

"Sure. Although you might get bored."

"Me? Never. What are you going to paint? I mean I suppose you're going to paint the pond."

Johnny described in detail the image he wanted to capture.

"Can I pose as the old man on the bench?" Rachael's enthusiasm was captivating.

"Sure. If you can wait until I can pencil in that part?"

"I can. Besides, I'm in no hurry to leave."

"Are you still in school? Oh, wait, thirty-five, you'd certainly be out of school by now."

Rachael nodded her head. "I work. But today's Friday, remember? I already worked my shift and I don't go back to work until Monday."

"And what do you do, Miss Rachael?"

"I'm a nurse, an RN in the emergency room over at the hospital."

"Really?"

"Yeah, and I do fashion modeling on the side."

"Great! Two jobs; you must be rich."

"Right. I'm so rich it isn't even funny. And how about you? Do you still work? You're not old enough to be retired."

"Well, I paint, I make custom jewelry, I do a few other things, and I'm fairly well invested in the stock market."

"You're a busy bee, Johnny More."

"At times." Johnny placed his canvas onto his easel as he spoke. "Here we go," he said.

"Tell me when you want me to sit on the bench," Rachael said, moving just behind Johnny's left side.

"Good deal," Johnny said. In a matter of seconds he caught the scent of Rachel's perfume. Although it was intoxicating, he made no comment about it; it would have sounded too . . . forward, and he would not offend his new friend. And after all, he was . . . sort of old enough to be her father. Well, almost. But even more than that, he hated the moniker, "dirty old man," and he was *not* going to let that title be heaped on him this night, or ever.

They made small talk as Johnny worked. He turned to look back at her on one occasion and was surprised to see how close she was to him. They stared at one another for a moment, prompting Rachael to move backward slightly. "I'm sorry; was I getting too close?" she asked.

The answer in Johnny's mind was anything but what he said. "It's okay. No problem. You're good." Swallowing hard, he turned back to his painting; he shut his eyes for a moment; he could still see her face; she was utterly gorgeous.

After ten minutes Johnny had finished the preliminaries and was ready to have Rachael sit on the bench. "How's this?" she said, slumping down slightly.

"Good. Now turn up the collar of your coat. I don't want the old man to look girly. Yeah, that's perfect."

Rachel sat very still until Johnny announced that he was done.

"Already? So, you won't be applying any paint tonight?"

"No. I'll go home and fool with it until I'm ready to paint."

"And when will that be?"

"Tomorrow night, or the next day."

"Hum."

"Hey, Rachael. You know what; I'd like to buy you some coffee or something for helping me. Would that be good with you? I mean you could drive your car to the restaurant if you want."

Rachel looked at her watch. "I don't have my car here. I walked from my apartment."

"Oh, well, that's okay. We can make it another time. Maybe I'll see you hear again sometime."

"No, that's not what I meant, I—"

"—I'll tell you what. You know where Brad's Pit Barbeque place is?"

"Yeah, around the corner," Rachael said, pointing her thumb back over her shoulder.

"I'll meet you there." With that they began to walk up the grassy knoll toward the street where Johnny's car was parked. "There I am," Johnny said, pointing at his one year old Mercedes.

"Nice car," Rachael said. She paused in thought as Johnny was placing his painting materials into the trunk.

"What the hell, Johnny," she began, "I'll just go with you to Brad's. I mean, it's not like you're going to attack me or anything. Besides, I can probably kick your ass, you being as old as you are, and—"

"—Right; you most likely being a pink belt and all."

They both laughed as Johnny was opening her door.

"Thank you," Rachael said, with a rising high pitched voice.

"Coffee," Rachael said to the waitress.

"Make that two."

"Cream and sugar?"

They both agreed on just cream.

After a pause, Johnny asked a question that he had begun to wonder about. "I hope you don't take this wrong, or think that I'm being nosey or something, but are you married? Or, do you have a boyfriend or anything? "I mean—"

Rachael looked only mildly puzzled. "Why do you ask?"

"Because I don't feature getting my old ass beat up if someone significant in your life passes by and happens to see us sitting here together."

"Well, first of all I'm not married, now. I mean I was, but he was killed Afghanistan."

"Oh, no; I'm so sorry to hear that."

"It's okay. I'm more or less over it now. Over the shock of his death that is. I'll never be over him."

Johnny wanted to say other things to her but she didn't give him the chance. "As for a boyfriend, you don't have to worry about getting beat up, because I haven't dated anyone in close to a year. So, there's no one in my life now—just you."

Johnny didn't know whether to laugh, kiddingly pat his hair back with his hand and blink his eyes, or take an aspirin to thin his blood to prevent a sure coronary.

"I mean, I don't have many friends, male friends that is. I've sort of shied away from most all men."

"So what made you be so friendly to me? I mean I was a total stranger."

"I don't know. You just looked sort of . . . nice. And you were carrying an easel. I mean most killer-rapists don't often walk around with easels and canvasses."

Johnny laughed. "It all makes sense," he said.

"So anyway, Johnny, what's the next step with your painting?"

"Well, I'll go home, perfect the drawing, and then I'll go back down to the pond to begin the color process. It will most likely take a week or two to complete, maybe longer."

"And what will you do with it then?"

"Give it to you," Johnny said, without hesitation.

"I'm sure."

"I'm serious."

"Why would you do that?"

"Because I don't have very many female friends. In fact, I haven't dated in a long time, so there's no one in my life now—just you."

Johnny said those words intending to mimic Rachael's previous witty statement that she had no one—just him. And they did both manage to laugh, but Rachael's eyes told another story, one that Johnny couldn't quite grasp. Five minutes later Rachel arose and placed her coat over her shoulders. "Time to call it a night," she said.

Johnny stood, threw down a ten dollar bill, and motioned for Rachael to head first for the door. "Can I drive you home? It's getting quite dark."

"No thanks, Johnny. I like to walk."

Johnny was mad at himself. Something he had said had changed her entire continence. He was sure of it. But he would say nothing about it, even though he sensed this would be the last time he would see her. They stopped just in front of Johnny's car.

"Well, it was a pleasure to meet you, Rachel. May our paths cross again someday—at least once so I can give you your painting."

Rachael then did something quite unexpected: she walked up to Johnny and embraced him; not as one would embrace a lover, but as a one would embrace a long-time friend. "I'll see you soon, Johnny-Johnny More," she said. Then she turned and walked into the night.

Johnny was finding it quite difficult to get Rachael out of his mind. He didn't visualize their being involved in some sort of wild romance. He couldn't put his finger on why she had become so lodged in his brain, but she was there in his dreams that night, during the following day, and back in his dreams the following night.

The artist finished his drawing early on the second day; he would travel down to the pond this evening to start the painting once promised to Rachael, but was now destined to go to . . . he knew not where.

With his easel, canvas, and full box of oils he set off on the short ride to the pond. He found himself wishing Rachael would be there on the bench when he reached the pond, but when he got there the bench was empty. He tried to shrug it off. "Why would she be here?' he said aloud.

He slowly went to work setting up his canvas; he placed his paints and pallet on the flat lid of a trashcan near the bench. Then, as was his custom, he stared long at the canvas. Finally, he filled his brush with the first color he would use; he steadied his hand, and began.

"Sorry I'm late," said a soft feminine voice behind him. He knew without turning that it was Rachael.

"Well, I didn't think—"

"If I'm going to be the recipient of this masterpiece, I'm going to be here to see it slowly come to life."

Johnny grinned and shook his head ever so slightly.

Rachael, not wanting to disturb the artist, opted to remain more or less silent as Johnny wielded his brush. Slowly, the still life drawing began to come alive. She could remain silent no longer. "You are amazing Johnny More!"

Johnny didn't hesitate. "What's amazing is the fact that for some reason you have inspired me to put everything I have into this . . . this work of art."

"Really?"

"Absolutely. And do you have a place in mind where you're going to hang it?"

"Well, I haven't even thought about it. But, I know one thing. When you're done, I want you to come to my house and I want you to tell me where I should hang it.

"That's a deal," Johnny said.

For the next four days Johnny and Rachael met at the pond. When needed, Rachael posed as the old man on the bench; she moved things for Johnny when it would have been awkward for him to do so, and she and Johnny talked about everything under the sun whenever a break seemed warranted. On the fifth day Rachael didn't show and Johnny's stomach churned as he pondered all the bad things that could have happened to take her away from him. But then his cell rang; it was Rachael saying that she was asked to do a double shift and that she would sleep the following day, adding that she would be there that next night. "Thank God for cell phones," he said to her just before they finished conversing. Then he remembered that he could have called her as she also had given him her number.

Rachael was there on the following night; it was finishing night. Together they sat on the bench. Johnny marveled at the job he had done. Not in a haughty way. Rather, he was amazed that Rachael, a girl he barely knew, had inspired him to do everything that he had done. And Rachael was overwhelmed. Overwhelmed that she was a part of such a work of art; and overwhelmed even more that she was to be the recipient of Johnny's work.

The moon shone high as Johnny and Rachael slowly made their way up to where Johnny's car was parked.

"When should I give it to you?" Johnny asked. "Do you want it now? I mean it can dry at your house as easily as anywhere else."

"Oh, no. Not now. Tonight I need to sleep. But tomorrow I want you to come to my house for dinner. And then we'll pick the place where it will hang."

"Sounds perfect," Johnny said. "There's only one catch."

"What catch? What do you mean?" Rachael's voice sounded abnormally strained.

"I don't know where you live."

Rachael closed her eyes for an instant. Then she raised her hand and pointed to the high-rise directly across the street from where they were standing. "Fifth floor, Suite Number One."

"Of course," Johnny said, and they both laughed.

"Hay, how do you think I knew when you were down there? I could see you—and your car."

"You're a tricky little kid, Miss Rachael."

"You can never be too cautious," Johnny More.

"Indeed, Rachael, Rachael . . . ahhhh—"

"—Oh, I'm sorry, Johnny, I never did mention my last name, did I?"

"No, you didn't. I thought it might have been part of your disdain for men. I mean, like it would be giving away too much of yourself if you told me your last name."

"Okay, I admit it; that's exactly what it was. But, you're my Mr. Johnny More now, I mean you've got my cell number, you know where I live, and you now know that my last name is Rose."

"Rachael Rose. Of course. Tricky you. What's more, you're a rose of a girl, too. Make that a rose of a woman."

"I think that's a compliment."

"It is," Rachael Rose.

"Tomorrow night then, at, say, seven?"

"The painting and I will be there."

Johnny More thought about Rachael Rose the rest of that night; and he dreamed of her as well. He couldn't say why he was so enthralled with her. They weren't lovers. They would never be lovers. Besides, she was too young for him. Well, maybe not; but he was too old for her; that was for sure. Well, almost. "This whole thing is so damn stupid," he sighed aloud. Finally, his eyes fluttered and a moment later he was asleep.

At 7:01 p.m. Johnny was at Rachael's door. He swallowed hard when his eyes fell upon her. Her hair was beautiful, and long; her face looked as though it had been molded by a modern-day sculptor, and on the plaque below that sculptor's work appeared the words, "The most beautiful girl in the world."

"Hi," Johnny said. It wasn't a cleaver salutation.

"Right on time; I like that," Rachael said. But Johnny didn't hear her; he was too busy trying to tame his wildly beating heart when he saw what she was wearing: a white sash that criss-crossed her breasts and was tied down around her waist in a bow just above her slightly exposed stomach, and below hung a silky red skirt that dropped to just above her stylish red leather shoes.

"Wow," Johnny said, as though not realizing what he had said.

"What?"

"Oh. Sorry. It's just that you look so damn gorgeous."

"Well, thank you. It's been a long time since anyone said something like that to me."

"Ah, well, here it is," Johnny said. He didn't want to dwell too long on the compliment train. He knew that sort of thing could backfire on a man.

"Okay, set it down right there and I'll give you a tour of the place. We'll sort of put our heads together as we go and we'll come up with a great place for it to hang."

Rachael's apartment was spacious, decked out with well chosen modern furniture; yet it was warm, with an array of both real and synthetic flowers enhancing every room they visited.

"Ah," Johnny said upon entering her bedroom, "I think our picture has found a home." He pointed to the wall opposing her queen-sized bed.

"You're kidding. Not in a more prominent place like the living room or dining room?"

After a slight hesitation Johnny said, "Of course it will be your ultimate choice, but it would mean a lot to me if I knew you might be looking at my work at the end of a hard day; and in the morning when you opened your eyes, and I was . . . I mean my painting was the first thing you saw just before rising to meet the new day."

"How beautiful! I'm sold. My painting will hang right there before the day ends tomorrow—frame and everything."

"It's a deal then," Johnny said, extending his hand.

"Deal," Rachael said.

They heard a sudden "ding" coming from the kitchen.

"That's the dinner bell. Come on and sit in the dining room while I pour the wine. You drink wine?"

"I do, Rachael Rose."

Rachael and Johnny drank their wine amidst small talk, at first, but their conversation soon turned to a subject that would open the way to an even closer relationship: the story of their lives—from their births, to date. But, when Rachael had finished her story, she stopped. She would serve dinner and then it would be Johnny's turn.

"I see you're a chef," Johnny said before allowing himself to experience his lamb chops, mashed potatoes, and broccoli; and that was not to mention the preliminary French onion soup and light salad topped with an excellent vinaigrette dressing."

"It was the least I could do after receiving such an exquisite painting."

"Hell, I'm thinking of filling your walls with my work!"

"Then I'll live here as long as you're doing it."

They laughed and at Rachael's behest Johnny began his own life story.

"So, both of our mates died, Johnny," Rachael said when Johnny was done. Odd, isn't it? I mean was it some sort of omen or something that we would one day meet?"

Johnny looked into Rachael's expressive eyes from across the table. "I don't know," he softly replied. And he certainly didn't know how to take her last comment. Did she mean that it was just a coincidence, or did she mean that they were destined to meet, and that their meeting would be the beginning of a long and beautiful relationship? Although it was against his better judgment, Johnny More would risk a question that had suddenly begun to plague his brain, knowing that if he was wrong it might cost him their relationship.

Rachael, I mean, I'm sorry all to hell if I end up ruining our . . . our friendship, but is there a place somewhere in your brain, or better, your heart, that says you think it's possible that . . . that—"

"—That it's possible that we might end up having a relationship closer than . . . than just being friends?"

Johnny swallowed hard. He couldn't speak, mainly because his voice box had just abandoned him.

"Is it possible for you, Johnny?"

"Oh, my God, Rachel, of course it is, but—"

"—But what?"

"I mean, I'm almost—"

"—You're almost old enough to be what? My father?"

"Almost, but . . . well . . . not really." Johnny couldn't hold back a small grin as he spoke. But Rachel was not in the least hesitant. Her grin was wide and beautiful as she said, "'Almost, but not really,' makes it a 'no,' and that 'no' makes us a possibility, Johnny. And that possibility makes it . . . makes us . . . a fact, Johnny More."

They didn't rush around the table to meet with desperately open arms, there to embrace one another with hot kisses, there to madly rush into the bedroom, to tear at one another's clothes until they were naked, to press their bodies together in love's first passionate embrace.

This was Johnny More, this was Rachael Rose, neither of whom felt forced to do the obvious; that would come in time. For now, Johnny simply moved around the table, pulled a chair up to Rachel's side, and reached for her hands, which she gladly offered to him.

"Would your husband approve, Rachael?"

"I'm not sure; would your wife?"

"You know, I just don't know. But I do know neither of them are with us any longer; it's just you and me now, and all I know is that I have not been able to get you out of my mind ever since the first moment I saw you. And as far as I'm concerned, if I can give you my love, and you can give me yours for . . . for even a little while, than I, at least, will be able to die a happy man no matter when that time comes. And I never thought I would be saying that to another woman, Rachael . . . not ever."

"I can reply to what you have just said by simply saying, yes, yes, and yes. And I can add nothing to what you have said, Johnny, other than to say that I began to fall in love with you the very first moment you lifted your charcoal to your canvas. And that was *before* you told me you would give me your finished work."

They both laughed at her words, and they spent the rest of the evening talking about their goals and aspirations, and their plans on how they might pursue those aspirations together, hand in hand, heart with heart, with laughter and joy, each knowing that the other would be loved beyond their wildest dreams.

It was two months almost to the day that Rachael was called to travel to Sacramento for at least a week, maybe longer. It had to do with receiving her credential as a nurse practitioner. A finalization action she called it. After that she would spend two days with her aunt on her mother's side and her long time girlfriend who lived nearby. And then she would return to her nursing job, her home, and Johnny.

Johnny wished he could travel with his new love but he wouldn't even ask, feeling that she needed to girl-bond. He drove Rachael to the airport the next day and thought about her every minute during the arduous bumper to bumper journey home.

The days of her absence were almost unbearable for Johnny. He had been with her day and night ever since the day he gave her his painting. She called him to say goodnight every night they were apart; it keep him relatively peaceful. Into the second week he received her call telling him that she would be coming home in two days. Two days later he felt his heart jump as she walked through the door of the waiting room at the airport. It was as though they had not seen one another for months, so joyful was their embrace.

Their trip home was long, but the traffic didn't bother either of them as they had much to tell one another. During a lull in their conversation Johnny looked over at Rachael and saw that she was looking out her side window; her head was resting back on her headrest.

"Tired?" Johnny asked.

"Some."

"I really missed you."

"I know. I didn't like being away from you for so long."

Johnny just smiled. He knew exactly how she felt.

They stayed together that night. They made love and moments later Johnny began a conversation, but he soon realized that Rachael had fallen into a deep sleep. He would not disturb her.

The next morning Rachael readied herself for work while Johnny made breakfast. "You look sexy in your nurses' uniform," Johnny said as Rachael sat to join him at the breakfast table. Her smile was warm but she made no reply.

"You excited about being a full-fledged nurse practitioner?"

"It's what I always wanted to be. At least I won't have to work in the emergency room too much longer."

Johnny sensed that from Rachael's short answers of late there was something on her mind, but for some reason he was reluctant to ask her if everything was alright. A short while later she arose saying that she needed to get to work earlier than usual. They kissed goodbye and a moment later Johnny was alone.

"Okay, there's something on your mind," Johnny said later that night. He couldn't accept the fact that their once robust conversations had suddenly turned into almost no conversations at all.

"You've changed a bit since you came back from Sacramento. What happened while you were there?"

Rachael looked long at Johnny. He sensed sorrow in her eyes.

"I don't know," she said.

"Not good enough."

Rachael shifted nervously in her chair. "Maybe we should just leave it alone. I'll be back to normal in a day or so."

"Okay, but I was just wondering; we've talked of marriage, haven't we?"

"Yes."

"And doesn't that mean that we should be all about sharing things that are on our minds?"

"Yes."

"Okay."

Several long moments of silence passed.

"Okay, Johnny, I'll be honest with you."

"Yes?" Johnny felt a sickening wave rush through his body; he knew there was something very wrong. He feared what he would hear next.

"I had several long talks with both my Aunt Jenny, and Alice, my best girl friend."

"So, between the three of you it was decided that our relationship can't work, because of our age difference, and therefore you decided that you no longer love me—however much you loved me."

"Come on Johnny, don't do that."

Johnny waited in silence.

"Okay, the crux of our conversation did have to do with our age difference."

Here it comes, Johnny said to himself.

"I'm thirty-five and you're fifty two."

Johnny just nodded.

"And that's okay—now."

"But?"

"Well, twenty years from now I'll be fifty-five, and you'll be seventy-two."

There were a lot of things Johnny could have said, things ranging from sarcasm to outright anger over Rachael's sudden "realization." He thought they were past all of that; that it didn't matter. But Johnny just looked at his disappearing lover and remained silent.

"Look, Johnny, I love you, and there is no one else. But, as we both know, you have a troubled heart, which means that I might lose you any time, meaning that you might not even make that twenty year marathon."

"And?"

"And I don't think I can take the loss of yet another husband, especially when it could happen at any time."

Johnny thought of a huge list of possible replies: that could happen to anyone, at any time; we could still have a beautiful life for as long as we were together; either one of us could get into an accident at any time, just like anyone else . . . and on it could go.

Instead, Johnny More just nodded his head as though he understood and agreed with everything she had said. "Okay, Rachael," he finally began, "I understand your reasoning. And you know what, I totally agree with you. It was a foolish thing to begin with, this relationship of ours. It shouldn't have happened in the first place."

"Are you giving up, Johnny? How can you give up so easily?"

Johnny felt irritated. "What is this, a test or something? What am I supposed to say? 'Oh, Rachael, please love me enough to want to spend the rest of your life with me.' Or maybe I'm supposed to dream up something to say that will cause you to break down and reconsider your decision to break up? Is that what you were hoping for? I mean, why should I have to do that, Rachael? You know that I love you and want you to be with me forever. Do you really want me to beg you?"

Two tears dropped from Rachael's eyes. "It's just so hard to know what to do, Johnny. God, I've already lost one man."

"Really? Is it really that hard, Rachael?"

Rachael lowered her eyes."

"Hey, little girl; it's really not so hard to know what to do. As a matter of fact, you don't have to do anything; I'll do it all for you."

Johnny arose from his chair as he spoke.

Rachael looked up at Johnny as though to say, "What are you going to do?"

"I'll simply walk out the door. You won't have to do or say anything. How easy is that?"

"You would do that?"

"I would, I could, and I will. And it's not because I don't love you, because I do, more than anything. In plain English, I'm going to call it quits because I do love you. Listen, Rachael Rose, I'm not one to hem and haw around when it comes to breaking off something that's not meant to be. I literally hate the thought of ending a relationship by piecemealing it—a little at a time. You do this, and I'll do this, and we'll see if this or that happens, if this or that works. Besides that, it's obvious that you don't love me enough to prevent our age difference from being a deciding factor in our relationship. I guess your aunt and your girlfriend know you better than I do. Good for them; they just saved you, Rachael."

Rachael was determined to meet his harsh words head on. "Do I have a say in this matter, Johnny?"

"You've already had your say, Rachael. The very fact that you said our relationship might not be one you would want over the long haul is enough to tell me that we were not meant to be together, even in the short haul."

With that Johnny More began to gather up the meager amount of belongings he had brought to Rachael's house during their short—affair. And Rachael? She just sat there in silence, which was another indicator to Johnny that he was doing the right thing.

When Johnny reached Rachael's front door he turned to face the woman he had loved from the first moment he had gazed upon her. "Goodbye, my sweet Rachael," he said. "Never forget that I loved you—more than anything in the world."

Rachael, with tears in her eyes and on her cheeks, opened her arms to embrace the man whom she obviously must not have loved enough to physically prevent his departure.

But Johnny, with silent tears in his own eyes, turned from her arms, and a moment later he was gone.

A week passed, then two. And as the days continued Johnny became more and more depressed. He knew he was destined to be alone—now and forever. Rachael had not attempted to contact him. Not by home phone, by cell, or otherwise. And he would never dream of contacting her; to do so would have been like . . ." Oh, please love me Rachael. Please ask me to come back." If he did that she would have looked at him with scorn.

As he laid there in his bed one night into the third week, a thought came to him: he would begin again; he would recreate his life as it was the day before he met Rachael Rose. From that point on he would live as though nothing had happened—as though Rachael had only been a dream. That very next evening he would gather up a new canvas, his easel, and a charcoal pencil. He would go down to the pond and he would recreate the same painting he had painted before, only this time he would keep the painting for himself. What's more, this time the man on the bench would be him. And if he wanted to he would one day paint a picture of an artist painting a picture of the pond. Maybe he'd even turn it into a summer scene with flowers all about, and a bright shining sun reflecting on the pond instead of a dreary winter scene.

The following evening, with a mild sense of joy in his heart, Johnny parked on the street above the pond and slowly made his way down the grassy hill. He would not turn to look up at Rachael's apartment window. As far as he was concerned Rachael had moved away. He set up his easel and canvas, looked long at the sight before him, and began to draw. But it was not long before his thoughts turned to the girl he had loved. A lump slowly began to form in his throat. He could pretend no longer. His eyes began to well and his tears began to fall, although he would not utter a sound.

Johnny finished his drawing then slowly walked to the empty bench. "I guess I should be thankful for the time I had with her," he quietly whispered, gazing now at the drawing he had done. It was the same scene he had done for Rachael. Then he realized that he had forgotten to draw the man on the bench—the old man that would now be him.

"I love your drawing," said a gentle voice behind him.

"Rachael!" he said as he spun about on the bench. His smile was wide and his heart was pounding with joy.

But Rachael was not there. No one was there.

A gnawing pain suddenly filled his chest. He tried to swallow but it was almost impossible. With an aching heart Johnny collected the things he had brought and turned toward the grassy hill. It seemed steeper than ever before as he made his way up to its summit. He couldn't help it. He looked up at Rachael's window. Her light was off. She was gone, gone forever.

Johnny paused as he neared the sidewalk. The pain lingered in his chest. He opened his trunk and placed his painting material inside. Suddenly, his chest began to throb in earnest; shooting pain began to travel up and down his left arm; his jaw began to ache. Then everything went dark . . .

Fortunately, two young men on bicycles saw Johnny fall just before they passed his car. The call to 911 and the trip in the ambulance to the entrance of the emergency room took less than ten minutes. Johnny was lucky; the hospital was only four blocks away.

Johnny's eyes fluttered as he was being wheeled down the hall en route to the emergency room. Lights on the ceiling and strange faces was all he could see. Where was he? What was happening to him?

"Johnny!" came a strangely familiar voice. "Hold on, Darlin, I'm here; I'll always be here. Hold on Johnny, please hold on."

Johnny More looked up at Rachael and smiled a weak smile. He raised his hand slightly and felt her hand grasping his own. "I've got you," he heard her say as they were transferring him to the emergency room bed.

Tubes and needles and masks and things being stuck on his naked chest dominated Johnny's world now. In and out of consciousness, and pain, and then numbness, and all the while Johnny's half opened eyes saw Rachael's face came into focus and then she was gone again . . .

"Come on, Johnny. Hold on, you can do it. For me, Johnny, do it for me . . . so we can be together again. I can't go on without you, Johnny. I know that now; I knew it all along; I just wanted you to call—"

"Excuse me, Ray," the doctor said as he began his work on the patient before him. Rachael moved but only enough to give the doctor the room he required. She would not let go of Johnny's hand.

Johnny suddenly opened his eyes. "Hi . . . little girl," he said, trying his best to smile.

Rachael's heart skipped several beats. "Hi, sweetheart," she said with a wide smile of her own. "I almost lost you."

Johnny couldn't see the tears in her eyes as she spoke. "We tried, Doll, didn't we?" he said.

"It never ended, Johnny. We just took a little vacation from one another—that's all."

"Yes, and I missed you so much that I guess it made me sick, and—" Johnny's words were suddenly cut short. His EKG screen began to display a grossly irregular beat.

"Johnny!"

"I . . . I . . . can't . . . breathe—"

"Hold on, Johnny! Hold on!"

Although it was her job, Rachael reluctantly moved aside to allow the shorthanded team to work on her Johnny. She couldn't think. Her jaw tensed; she closed her eyes. "Don't go, Johnny, don't leave me," she repeated again and again.

The constant sound of the EKG's flat line penetrated her brain. Another nurse brought her a chair then helped her sit. Rachael's hands were shaking and she would have passed out had another nurse not handed her a cold washcloth.

"Would you like to be alone with him?" her teammate said once she saw Rachael would not faint.

"Thank you," was all Rachael could say. It was as though her brain was paralyzed, as though she had been the one that died.

With the curtain drawn, and as though by rote memory, Rachael set to work wiping Johnny's face and smoothing back his ruffled hair. She pulled off the wires and unplugged his IV, and then she covered his naked body with a sheet, but not his face—as long as she could see his face he was—still with her. Taking her chair she took his still warm hand and placed it to her lips. "This happened because of me, Johnny. I'm so, so, sorry. I wanted to call you, I promise you I did. I wanted to tell you that I didn't care how old you were, and that I loved you for who and what you are, my Johnny. I looked at your painting every night and I cried myself to sleep because you were not there with me. I was so *stupid* for listening to anyone, or anything, other than my own heart. My heart was filled with love for you all along, Johnny; I loved you every minute of the time we were apart.

The lump in Rachel's throat prevented her from speaking further. She lowered her chin to her chest and quietly sobbed. It was all she could do . . .

"Excuse me, Nurse," said a voice forty minutes later. It was the coroner with orders to move Johnny's body down to the morgue.

Rachael looked up. "Alright," she sobbed. Still in a state of shock, she watched as Johnny's body was moved onto the gurney that would take him away. "Johnny?" she sobbed when she saw the coroner pull the sheet over her Johnny's dear face. She followed the coroner out of the emergency room, but she would not follow him down to the morgue. She watched him being wheeled down the long corridor until it finally curved off to the right. She took a long deep breath, then exhaled. Johnny More, her dear and wonderful Johnny, was gone forever.

It's not for you to know how long ago those events took place. Maybe it was twenty years ago, maybe longer; then again, it might have been just a few months ago. But, what I can tell you is that if you happen to have a pond somewhere near where you live; go there sometime, around sundown on a blistery winter day. And if you're lucky you just might see a woman with a canvas and an easel, painting in constant repetition the most beautiful pictures you will ever see of a bright moon shimmering across the surface of that lovely pond, a pond surrounded by a grove of barren trees each eagerly awaiting the warmth and beauty of the coming spring. And if you look close you'll see an old man in each of those pictures, sitting on a bench near the pond as though contemplating his life and a love that you know will never die. And if you look carefully at the bottom right corner of each painting, you will see, very lightly printed, the words— "For my Johnny."

Unions

I'll begin by telling you that I have been in a union ever since I was twenty. That's like maybe a hundred years ago. So, don't say that I don't know what I'm talking about when it comes to this subject.

For your information there are two distinct types of unions: government unions (Federal, State, County, and City unions), and private unions: these unions represent workers from industries not run by a Federal, State, County, or City agency.

There is a huge difference between these two types of unions: government unions are subject to the particular governing bodies they work for, who are, in turn, theoretically subject to the public for whom they ultimately work. Private unions interact with the private industries for which their members work.

Bottom line: when contracts expire, government run unions "dicker" with government appointed "higher-ups" who supposedly represent "the People." Of course, these unions and those "higher-ups" don't give a shit about "the people for whom they all work." All they care about on both sides of that "argument" is finding a way to rob "the People" of enough money to get what they want. Private unions, on the other hand, "haggle" with the owners of the industries for which they work. In other words, private businesses have a finite amount of money to bargain over, as opposed to government unions who deal with the public which they (the government unions) think has an inexhaustible supply of money to give them.

Another huge difference between these two types of unions is the fact that with government unions it is almost impossible to fire a worker. For example, no matter what the hell a teacher does (maybe short of killing a fellow worker or a student) that teacher cannot be deprived of his or her status as a teacher. You may not know this, but there are literally hundreds of teachers—who have been barred from teaching for a number of reasons—yet they are allowed to go to their schools, there to waste the day away until it is time to go home. These teachers, because they can't be fired, still receive their paychecks, and their benefits. And guess who pays for all of that? Could it be you? What a fucked up system!

Conversely, private union workers, although it is sometimes difficult to do, can be fired for the improper things they might do. And they aren't given daily paychecks after they leave unless they are entitled to their pension. And sometimes even their pensions end up in jeopardy.

I have been with the S.E.I.U. most of my life, but the company I worked for is a private company. (The S.E.I.U. handles both entities.) Whenever I got a raise the company and the union negotiated the contract. If the company could not afford to give us a raise, it showed us, on paper, in black and white, why they could not afford to give us a raise. I can remember times when the company I worked for was on the brink of bankruptcy and our union members voted to maintain the status quo to help save the company from disaster. Do you think a government union would do that? Fat chance!

I taught in a public school for a while. When it came time to negotiate a new contract, the other teachers and I paid little attention to what was going on because we knew we would automatically get almost everything the negotiators asked for. And even in places where you see teachers picketing and screaming their stupid heads off about how bad things are for them, they know they will eventually get what they want—even though their City, County, State, or Federal Government is so far under water it's frightening. (Hello Chicago.)

As for you union haters, just know that when you are discussing unions—as you are sipping your wine around your table of union haters—all unions are not alike. Some unions are a blessing. Without them workers would be bullied and generally kicked around, forever under the threat of being fired, even for petty things. Their jobs would never be secure, even if they were among the best workers a given industry could find. Why? Because it is human nature for a private company to make all the money it can possibly make, often at the expense of its workers. And that's okay, as long as there is a force looking out for the wellbeing of the workers. What's more, some people in management tend to dislike certain workers, and they find nothing wrong with making life miserable for them. Unions are able to help alleviate that condition. And that's a good thing.

But that doesn't make it all right for a union to bankrupt an industry when trying to get everything it wants. Sometimes a union has to be every bit as fair as they want the businesses they work for to be. By that same token, it certainly isn't right for government unions to screw the American public like they have done for so many years. Yet, even government workers need representation.

After all, someone has to go to bat for those workers. If it was up to me, I'd have the government hire a private firm to do its negotiating for them, a pro public firm that would not be prone to automatically cave in to every union demand they are hit with. But, of course, very few people would agree with me. And things will carry on—as usual.

In some ways I'd like to see every worker in the United States belong to a union that really cared about its members, along with the businesses they dealt with. As I said, all workers need representation. Then again, that would be like asking for graft and corruption and greed (on both sides) to vanish into the cosmos. How plausible do you think that would end up being? The big unions that pushed to get Obama elected is proof of what I've been saying. They pushed to get Obamacare enacted as well, and then they got Obama's permission to bail out of Obamacare when it came to the possibility of their having to participate in that catastrophe. What a fucking crock!

If unions would listen to what I am saying, instead of saying that I am full of shit, their decline, which they are now suffering, would make an about face and a true balance between workers and the businesses they work for would result. And that would be a good thing, and that goes for government unions as well.

The Press

When I was a young man I was rather a-political. My parents were Democrats. My father (at the age of five) and his family of nine immigrants appreciated being able to come here, although Ellis Island in 1905 was a scary place for them to go through. But all ten of them made it, and all ten eventually became citizens. (Their names are on the east facing wall of Ellis Island.) From the beginning they all erroneously attributed this American acceptance to the goodness of the Democratic Party and all it supposedly represented—in spite of the fact that a Republican was in office at the time. (New Yorkers really know what's what, don't they?

Time passed, I was born, grew, and finally reached voting age. The Democratic candidate was to be John Kennedy. It was a given that I would vote for him. He was Catholic (in other words a religious person), he was from Boston where my mother grew up (as did her relatives ever since the early 1600's); he was young, nice looking, and he had a Boston accident, as did half of my relatives. I mean, who else would I vote for?

Once Kennedy took office I loved everything he did and said. He was my idol. And the press agreed with me. Hell, everyone agreed with me. Even when he mismanaged the Cuban invasion and had to pay for it by being forced to toy with the Russians over the missile crisis, I still loved him. And then I began to study politics, and eventually I began to learn about Kennedy, the man, and I slowly began to move to the opposite side of the spectrum. Yet, all through the years the press clung to not only Kennedy but to the Democratic Party as well. (I should add that I met J.F.K. on two different occasions, and on one of those occasions I had a rather decent, uninterrupted, conversation with him.)

After Johnson, came Nixon, but the press held fast to its love affair with the Democratic Party, meaning its love affair with the left. Nixon was elected twice, the second time by a landslide, and of course the press hated every minute of each of his two terms—the second term even more that the first. They (the press) waited until the right time (Watergate) whereupon it pounced on "ol' Tricky" with everything it had. The Republicans, being the dumb asses they have always been—except during the Lincoln era, and for a while with Reagan—caved as they have always done, and the press was able to instigate that president's untimely departure, allowing Ford to finish out his (Nixon's) abandoned term. Then came Carter and the pathetic four year fiasco that followed.

It was now time for Reagan to run. During the entire campaign the news people (the talking heads) gave their full faith and support to Walter Mondale, each day optimistically enjoying their multiple orgasms in anticipation of a Mondale win. Unfortunately for the press, Reagan won, and he was able to outsmart that press for eight years. It killed the leftists to see a Republican conservative manage to remain in office for so long; they tried to "get" him but it was as though he was made of Teflon, and I know for a fact that many of those in the press hoped that the "Gipper" would die from the bullet he received as a result of an attempted assassination. But it was not to be, and Reagan lasted until the end of his term.

Unfortunately for the press, a Republican took over again (Bush the elder) and the leftists again found themselves wallowing in misery. Socialism had been stayed once again. Finally, Clinton took over, giving the leftist press new hope. Despite doing things any Republican would have been crucified for doing, Clinton lasted for eight years. Bush the younger battled the press for the following eight years, pissing off every liberal in the nation, including ninety per cent of the members of the press. Obama was then elected and the Democrats and the socialist left received the greatest boost in the history of the Democratic Party. And on it will go with Hillary Clinton, who, if she runs, will most likely win the election in 2016. And the collective daily orgasm of the press, in its pursuit of socialism, will go on.

Since this "ranting" was not meant to be a complete history of the presidency, I'll just say that the media has been, is now, and ever shall be dominated by a conglomeration of liberals and socialists, along with a huge hunk of people who think Democrats are the kindest, most charitable, most un-prejudice people on earth. Which is, of course, utter bullshit. In short, if it had to be said in percentages, the leftist press equals seventy-five percent of the media, the right, twenty-five percent. This is not a good thing for the American people. And it would not be good if it were it to be in the reverse: seventy-five per cent conservative, twenty-five percent liberal. The press needs to be unbiased. It's okay for commentators to comment as long as there is a balanced mixture of opinions. The rest of the press should concentrate on giving the American people the news, i.e. it should tell people what has happened, or what is happening, and nothing more. In other words, let the American people decide what to conclude regarding a given issue.

Personally speaking, do the above facts about the press piss me off? No, they don't. It's the way things are meant to be. After all, this country would be held back from its eventual collapse were it to be the other way around—were the right to be the dominant part of the media.

This brings me to a condition that utterly pisses off the liberal/socialist seventy-five percent: Fox News. If the left could get away with it, as one, it would have O'Reilly and the others assassinated. And I mean that literally. Of course it goes without saying that the left, were it to collectively read this book, and then be collectively interviewed, it would loudly proclaim that it would want to do no such thing. But, hey, remember, this is me writing this book. You can't snow me; I know better; I've been around too long.

The funny thing is Fox News, although a right leaning organization, tries its damndest to show both sides of whatever issue it is discussing. In the long run Fox's people usually dominate the conversation, but at least the other side is allowed to have its say, unlike what happens in the rest of the media. And that is the crux of what pisses me off: many of the seventy-five percenters are a bunch of morons ever willing to spout their side of an issue, and equally willing to say, "Screw the right; we don't care what they think, or say." As a result, seventy-five percent of the American people are perpetually kept in the dark on almost every issue worth debating. But, of course, that's nothing new. It's the way it's always been.

You want to know something? Ultimately, both the right and the left in the media are full of shit. The left is just full of more shit, that's all. By the way, I should confess that (with few exceptions) I can't stand to read newspapers and magazines any more. At least live television isn't as boring. And guess what else? If you get most of your news online you are, without a doubt, the most confused type of moron of them all. How the hell can you ever know if what you read online is the truth! At least on television you can get an idea of who is saying what. Tweet that fact to your dimwit, fanatic, cell phone friends!

And remember this: the media is geared to play to the audience it thinks it has. If Fox thought the majority of its listeners were socialists you'd see some big changes, and I mean right now! And if the networks and CNN and the rest of the morons thought their audiences were turning conservative you'd see changes you wouldn't believe. Think of it this way: the reason that Fox is so big is because that organization is the only major cable organization currently giving voice to both sides of every issue. Meaning the second half of the nation currently watching Fox is able to hear what the first half never hears. Baring that fact, our entire nation would be comprised of a giant ship of fools.

Personally, I don't like having to hear the socialist side every time Fox holds a discussion on a given topic. On the other hand, sometimes the left makes a decent point and I'm glad to alter my viewpoint on that particular point. But, you seldom get a chance to alter your opinion when all you watch are the liberal/socialist channels. I love it when I see someone shunning a Fox reporter when that would-be interviewee sees the Fox logo on the microphone of the interviewer. "Oh, you're from Fox. I hate Fox. I won't even talk to you." It just fortifies the fact that many people don't really want to know both sides of a given issue. Hey, you know what—don't watch Fox and be content to stay uninformed.

Obamacare

Obamacare is a ploy calculated to create both a socialist State, and to buy votes. Of course, socialism has never worked; what's more, it will never work. Consider: A country that even comes close to having a workable socialist system is a country that needs to have at least two of the following three factors present: 1) it needs to have a miniscule population, 2) it must have a valuable natural resource that is more or less inexhaustible, such as oil, and/or 3) it must be a country like Switzerland that has billions of dollars flowing into its banks on a daily basis; dollars that constantly accrue interest and fees from those who are willing to pay that country to securely hide their wealth. The United States does not fit into those narrow categories. Neither do ninety-five percent of the countries in the world. So, every time a country tries socialism, without two of these three variables being present, it fails.

So, what this ploy, called Obamacare, will do to our nation is foster socialism and thereby hasten its destruction. But what the hell, that's what you want, right? So, in the long run—you win. Congratulations! By the way, a word to the wise: It will take only one generation of time for the American public to forget what a magnificent medical care system we had before Obamacare took over. (And that's including the flaws the old system had.) The people who know this as a fact will die out, leaving an ignorant middle class to battle it out in order to stay alive in a system that the new middle class won't even know has turned to shit. And the lower class will jump for joy knowing that no effort on its part will be necessary to continue with its (grossly substandard) medical care. And the upper class will spend its money on what's left of the crème of the crop in terms of the medical care they will want and/or need. And the American public in total will surely suffer for having brought this catastrophe upon itself.

The following is the hidden explanation for why Obamacare was created:

Conniving socialist politicians (with Obama at their lead), espousing their usual rhetoric about how they just want to help the poor and the indigent, finally figured out the best way to create a socialist state. If they could control one sixth (or more) of our economy they would be able to eventually control our entire economy.

The ploy they knew would appeal to a great number of people— "helping the poor and the downtrodden in our society"—would be the catalyst that would help them (the socialists) take over our entire healthcare system. Playing on the sympathies of our Judeo/Christian majority, along with our black and brown population, the socialists knew that they could not lose that race. So, Obamacare was created and passed, albeit narrowly, without one Republican vote.

The socialists knew that once this was accomplished it would matter little whether the plan was successful; Obama and his cohorts were on their way to a single payer healthcare system, which is pure socialism, and nothing would be able to stop it. And the way I see it nothing will stop it.

So there you are, America. You got what many people warned you would get: a healthcare system doomed to fail, and an economic system destined to collapse. I realize that many of you were well meaning. After all, Christ said we should help the poor, feed the hungry, and care for the sick. However, he didn't say that we should do it by using the edicts of socialism. The fact is we were doing a damn good job accomplishing those admirable things using our capitalist system—compromised as it has been for lo these many years.

Just wondering. Did you ever see people dying on the streets of our country because they could not afford to get medical help? Or, because they were literally dying of starvation? If you said yes then you should have helped those people get the aid they needed because every one of them were entitled to go to the nearest emergency room or public (or private) assistance center constructed for just such emergencies. What's more, have you ever heard of 911? If they couldn't get help whose fault was it? Our healthcare system? Get real!

Just thought you'd like to know that just as the drug cartels in places like Colombia used to give money and food and other things to the poor of that country (in order to capture their minds and hearts, and thereby earn their unending support), the liberals/socialists in the U.S. have long ago learned to do the same thing, but in a far more subtle way. And more than half the country has fallen for it. Are you part of that half?

Two things you should read: 1) Rules for Radicals by Saul Alinsky, and 2) the narrative taken from Sunday, 07 September, 2008 Meet the Press, Obama interview. That's all I'll say about it.

Abortion

I'm not going to write a long article on abortion. I will merely make a few observations and let it go at that.

I heard a black congresswoman say that white people who are against abortion, are against it because they want to see more white people being born, because white births are in the decline. This is about the stupidest thing I've heard a congressperson say in the last . . . let's say . . . the last week!

First of all, it would make more sense for some white bigot to say that he or she is FOR ABORTION because 75% of the babies being aborted in this country are non-white. In other words, the more non-white babies are aborted the less non-white people there will be in this country. In any case, the declining number of white births in this nation is due to factors other than abortion.

As it is now, a pregnant woman has three choices: 1) to have the baby and keep it, 2) to have the baby and put it up for adoption, or 3) to abort the baby. I personally believe that the third option, abortion, should not be legal. Why? Because I do not believe a person has the right to take the life of another human being who is not an aggressor.

I'm tired of hearing people trying to argue that a baby, before it is born, is not a baby. Do they think that by calling it a fetus makes it a non-baby? I know this may be like a shocking revelation to some of you, but when one of them little bitty wiggly sperm things latches on to one of them little bitty egg things, life begins. And nothing the pro abortion advocates can conjure up in their little pea brains to deny that fact can make that reality a non reality.

Nevertheless, pro abortion advocates need to cling to their mantra that a fetus is not a human baby, that it is not a human life. If they do this they will be able to maintain their stance that the abortion team (the mother and the doctor performing the abortion) is not taking a human life, and that they are not killers. Of course, most of these killers know that they are killing a human being. It is the reason why so many women carry the guilt of what they have done to their graves—as well they should.

Isn't it odd that everyone is able to talk about the millions of people Hitler killed, but no one wants to talk about the hundreds of millions of babies killed by way of abortion throughout the world?

Let's face it, put into the language of truth, the so-called "Woman's right to choose" means the "Woman's right to murder, or not murder." Yeah, right, "Pro Choice." Hey, guess what? It still means the same thing: the right to murder or not to murder." Don't forget, we're not talking about one body here, we're talking about two bodies: the mother's body and her baby's body. So answer this: should a baby have the right to murder its mother if it could? Who would say YES? Do you see how the pro abortion advocates can never admit that the little thing pushing its way out of that dark cave is anything other than a fetus? In other words, it is not a human life until the last part of its body is free of that confounding fetus house. Strange; it looked the same just before it came out; it looked the same a week before that, and a week before that. In effect, to the pro abortion people, a baby becomes a baby when it's out of the mother, and its cord is cut. What a farce! Talk about a rationalization!

Rape. Pro abortion advocates are usually able to stump the anti abortion people when it comes to the question of rape. And I can sure see why. Having a baby inside of you because some sonofabitch forced himself on you is a terrible thing to have to endure. I'll tell you what, if I was a woman and I got raped by some rotten bastard, I'd want to see two things happen: the rapist on a slab in the morgue, and his baby out of me ASAP.

The only thing is, there would now be two victims: me AND the baby, a baby that did not ask for this to happen to it, or to me. So, I, being a onetime victim, am now going to become a victimizer, because I am now going to kill the living baby within me. In other words, I am willingly making the baby within me the victim, just like I was the victim when I got raped.

In short, in the case of rape, if you value human life, you should have the baby and either keep that baby (which I, personally, would not be able to do if I had been raped), or have the baby and then give it to a couple who has dreamed of having a baby of their own, but cannot. Thus, you would be making lemonade out of lemons. You would become a duel hero: a hero for bearing that burden for nine months, and a hero to the people who will receive the gift of a human life from you. I know it's easier said than done. But at least consider it.

Last, those of you who become pregnant one or more times out of wedlock (for whatever reason), and have had that baby (or those babies) aborted (for whatever reason), you should know that you, and those who performed that/

those abortion/s, have committed murder. You can try to spin that fact away all you want, but you will never be able to adequately do so. You are a murderer. Repent. And don't do it again!

The Trip

I was going to fly to Rome, then go on a cruise to Greece, Egypt, the Holy Land, and end up in England. But there was so much chaos going on at the time that I decided to see America instead—or at the very least the east coast of America.

I flew to Washington D.C., stayed in a hotel on Road Island Street, and for the next three days I walked the streets of our Capital. I saw nearly everything a person can see there—all the memorials, all the monuments, the Smithsonians, practically every building worth seeing, and every major cemetery. I then set out on a bus tour of D.C. which included Mount Vernon where I saw the bed upon which George Washington died, as well as his tomb. At Arlington Cemetery I saw Kennedy's grave and witnessed the changing of the guard, during which time some people in the crowd watching the event began talking, causing the guard to stop, turn, and tell them to shut the fuck up. Of course, he didn't use those exact words, but trust me the entire crowd became very quiet once he had finished chastising them.

The bus tour continued on, stopping at dozens of points of interest including Jamestown, Richmond, Gettysburg, Independence Hall in Philadelphia, Williamsburg, Harper's Ferry, and much more. From there the tour bus headed to New York City where we transferred to a cruise ship that took us up the Atlantic coast all the way to Nova Scotia, whereupon we slowly made our way south, stopping to see the sights in every State, from Maine to Massachusetts.

I'm telling you about this trip hoping to inspire you to take a similar trip. If you do it may change your prospective of this country: why it came into being, and why it became what it became. The only thing it won't do is tell you why it is the way it is now.

I may have told you that I taught school at one time. In fact, I taught every grade from the first grade to the twelfth grade. I've also given lectures on both the junior college and college level. On the high school level I taught both World and American history, which brings me back to the long trip I took in 2012. While on this trip I realized that you can teach all you want about a given subject, but you'll never quite be able to give it that spark of enthusiasm needed to make your subject come alive until you've been to the places your text books talk about. You can talk about Gettysburg, but until you stand on the field where Picket's charge took place, or stand on the hill where the Union soldiers dug in (the same hill that decided the war), but you will never be able to discuss those events with the same vigor as one who has been there. That goes for every historic place I visited. In effect, what I witnessed told me that everything that happened in our rather tumultuous history was worth it, because it made this country the greatest country in the world. The sad part is—I have little faith that it is going to last because the majority of people living here don't know a damn thing about it.

Take a trip before it's too late.

Cell Phones

This cell phone crap is getting ridiculous. Every place I go people are looking down smacking their stupid fingers on their cell phones-I-Phones-U-phones-screw-up-the-world-phones! Drive down the freeway and you can bet that you'll be able to count at least fifty people looking at their phones rather than at the road. (Have the person riding with you do the counting.) And most of them are young girls who are getting to be the worst freaking drivers in the universe. What's more, these girls are getting boulder and more violent by the day.

What I'll say next goes for the entire driving population of the United States. In case you didn't know it: At any given intersection, when two or more cars reach that intersection at the same time, THE PERSON ON YOUR RIGHT HAS THE FUCKING RIGHT-OF-WAY. For all you stupid ass teenagers, college graduates, young girls, et al, this means that the person on your right has the right to go first—if the two of you stop at an intersection at the same time. It does NOT mean that if the person on your right pauses for one thousandth of a second, you should say, "fuck it," and rush on across the intersection, figuring that he/she waited way too long to make up his or her mind to go.

The other day I stopped at an intersection some five seconds before the car on my left stopped. (In case you didn't catch what I just said about this—I had the right-of-way.) But, as I started across the intersection, the driver on my left decided to beat me to the punch. When I was half way across the intersection, the YOUNG GIRL DRIVER was forced to stop; otherwise she would have broadsided me. Instead of smiling, or waving at me indicating that it was her error, she began swearing out the window at me, and then she extended her middle finger out that window to accentuate her point.

I didn't swear back at her, and I didn't give her the finger like she did to me. Of course, I have to admit that I wanted to tear off her stupid finger then stick it up her stupid little . . . . but, I didn't; in fact I didn't do or say anything to her; I just kept on driving.

And then I began to wonder if people are like that to other people (especially me) because they think they can kick the other person's (my) ass, or because the other person is old, or . . . or what? I mean, yeah, I'm older than dinosaur crap, but most other drivers don't know how old I am because I wear a baseball hat and shades when I drive, and I don't have white sideburns, and my face isn't wrinkled. So, they don't know how old I am. Besides, people often tell me that I look a lot younger than I am (maybe about twenty-five.)

Bottom line: my advice to you is to be careful what you do and say to other people because they may look helpless, but they just might be deadly if provoked. They may even be prone to carry a loaded 45 caliber semi-automatic under their front seat. You know what I'm saying?

Back to the cell phones. Okay, I have cell phone. It costs me $80 a year, and has big numbers on it; not because I can't see; rather, it's because I don't have girl fingernails so I can't peck out a message using those tiny letters and numbers most people have on their cell phones. What's more, there are only about five people who know my cell phone number. Why? Because I don't like anybody, so I rarely give out my number. Oh, but you could have guessed that without me telling you, right? What's more, who would ever want to call a grumpy, mean, ol' sum-bitch like me?

I'll tell you what: you people let your dumb-ass bratty little kids talk on their cell phones all day, and before you know it the only way you're going to be able to have a conversation with them is by texting them, or by email, or by tweeting them (or whatever the hell you call it). You think heron is addictive! These phones are taking over the fucking world!

Don't be surprised when they figure a way to have real sex over the phone. When that happens you better be prepared to confiscate your eight year old's phone—pronto!—or you'll be grandparents long before you're fully prepared to suffer that role.

Remember this: the cell phone will be the cause of the death of human communication. The more that people become addicted to their cell phones, the less they will rely on face to face communication with one another. And that indeed will be a very dangerous condition for all of us.

Drugs

I used to sell drugs. No-no, I worked for a pharmaceutical company, a well known company in fact. It was my job to charm the nurses into letting me talk to their doctors, leave samples for them to give to their customers, and teach the doctors how to use the drugs my company manufactured—that is if they were willing to listen to me. I was lucky. Most of the docs in my territory did listen to me. Fact was I was able to save the lives of a lot of their patients by instructing them on how to administer our drugs to their patients. On more than one occasion I heard a doctor say, "I can't figure out why so many of my patients have died lately. I mean like your drugs are supposed to be among the best in the industry, and now people are dying from them."

As always, my answer would be, "Yeah, well you're killing them, Doc, because from what you have told me you're giving them the wrong dose." Or, "You're giving our drugs in combination with (so-and-so drug) and you're not supposed to do that because it makes their (heart, liver, etc) do this, or that, and that can kill them." And the doctor would laugh, and say, "Wooops," and they wouldn't prescribe those doses or that combination anymore. Oh well, at least they admitted their errors.

I remember the times when drug reps would cruise into a parking lot of a huge medical center, or a local

restaurant, and everyone would get out of their cars
and open their trunks, and whatever drug you needed
for yourself, your wife, or a family member would be
available for the taking (in sample form.) I'm not talking
about dangerous drugs; it was more often than not birth
control pills, antibiotics, or prescription cough medicines.
Dangerous? Yeah, but don't forget that we knew more
about these drugs than the doctors, and it was a given
that we would not give a drug to a family member if we
thought it could hurt them. That's sort of a bullshit spin
on the matter, but we all thought it was true at the time.
Anyway, I don't ever remember hearing of a detail man's
family member dying because of those antics.

I might add that my company was among the cheapest
companies in the industry. As a result, I seldom was able
to carry more drugs in my trunk than I was charted to
distribute to the doctors in my territory. In other words,
I did very little trading. And I was glad for it as I never
had to worry about getting caught giving out free drugs
or hurting anyone who might incorrectly take one of my
company's drugs. That fiasco took place over 45 years ago.
Nowadays, that sort of thing almost never happens. And
I'm glad because the drugs we now have on the market are
even more deadly than those available way back then.

While in college (prior to becoming a pharmaceutical
salesman) I hung around with a ton of different types of
people: students attending my college, friends from high
school, friends from others schools, and people I had met
from . . . wherever. As my life melted into the 1960's, more
and more people I knew were taking illegal drugs. I know
I'm going to sound like a freaking nerd to some of you ex
and current addicts, but I never became too interested in
taking any of the drugs that abounded during those years,

including marijuana. Maybe it was because I saw three of my best friends die of drug overdoses during that time. One of them was one of the greatest players of a certain instrument in the history of that instrument—before or since. Another was an absolutely brilliant doctor of psychology, and the third was a famous singer whose name I won't mention—and there's a chance you would know who that person was.

I couldn't drink much hard liquor either, mainly because it literally burned the living crap out of my stomach, and marijuana made my heart go into tachycardia every time I tried it. In short, it was easy for me to say to hell with both of them. Guess I was lucky.

I remember a friend giving me some marijuana seeds from Hawaii. They sat in my drawer for three or four years. Running across those seeds, I decided to plant them, more on a whim than anything else, and about month later a literal tree full of that crap came roaring up out of the ground in my back yard! I pulled off some green leaves, put them in the microwave, rolled them in cigarette paper and smoked it. I freaking almost died! What's more, I had hallucinations only dreamed about in the reveries of mushroom users.

That was the day I said to hell with it! I harvested a ton of leaves over the next few months with the intention of giving them to my stupid ass drug sucking friends—for free. (I truly had no intention of selling that stuff to anyone. And I never did. And I don't give a shit if you don't believe me.)

Finally, some grammar school kids were looking over the eight foot fence that separated our houses, and I hear this one kid say, "Hey, Mike, isn't that marijuana?" (The sixth graders were doing that DARE program at the time.)

"Nah, it just looks like it, but it isn't," I yelled back over to them.

That night I pulled up the entire bush. I cut it up and put it into two very large trash bags, and into the garbage can it went. I then placed my entire stash of nineteen *pounds* of ground up marijuana leaves into that trash can as well. How much would that be worth in today's market? The following morning the trash trucks came, and that was that. I've never even seen a blade of marijuana since that day. That was over 45 years ago.

Anyway, about two weeks later I got a card in the mail. It was from the rats and mice living in the dump where my "trash" went thanking me from the bottoms of their little hearts for my contribution to their continuing happiness.

Drugs today? Most young people think marijuana (among the other shit they take) is no big deal. They're even saying that about crack and the more dangerous things now available to them on the market. But you know what? They're full of shit! Those drugs are ruining more lives now than ever before. And they are turning our youth into a bunch of mindless idiots, and our eighteen to forty year old (plus) dimwits into a class of know nothing/do nothing losers, incapable of carrying on our traditions, which have, over the years, made great what has long been called, "The American Way." And by the way, the marijuana of today is around one hundred times more potent than it was in my day. And regardless of what some of the lamebrain so-called experts say—MARIJUANA IS ADDICTIVE!

I guess I've been lucky not even having the choice to become an alcoholic, or a drug addict, like so many of our citizens, citizens who I'm sure are now looked at as being American heroes, unafraid to venture out of their comfort zones. On the other hand, mill this around in your head:

Michael Blade

When the socialists in this country are taken over by the jihadists, or the Chinese, you will no longer be able to gulp down your alcohol until you drop each night, or suck your drugs to your heart's content, because in that new society those things will be very big no-no's. So much so that if you are caught indulging in one of your cherished habits, your heads may well be separated from your bodies, rendering you incapable of ingesting so much as a glass of water. A word to the wise: find a less life threatening habit.

Oh yeah, and good luck to the idiots in states like Colorado who can now consume marijuana legally. Of course you know that soon every state will be like Colorado, which means that those states are equally destined to become poverty stricken, slum infested, hellholes with crime rates so high it will be frightening.

So, hey Dude—suck your drugs to your hearts' content. But don't be surprised if one day your heart suddenly decides to stop because of it.

Who Is Right?

His name is Robert White. He is a Christian, a Roman Catholic to be specific. Told by the Bible to feed the hungry, aid the sick, visit the imprisoned, shelter the poor, clothe those who have no good clothes, he vowed to do those very things. When it comes to voting he always votes Democrat because he believes that Democrats are of the mind to follow those tenants (even though many of them aren't religious). He subscribes to the tenant that the government has the right to take from the rich in order to give to the poor. Robert knows that the "rich" are taxed at a rate of forty to fifty percent of their income, or more. He knows that this revenue comes from a small percent of our population, and that a huge percent of our citizens pay no taxes at all—except for the taxes they pay when they buy things. Robert also subscribes to the notion that people who can't take care of themselves have the right to expect the federal government to take care of them. Because of these notions, Robert champions every program the government has created/creates to do those things: food stamps, Social Security, Medicare, Medicaid, unending unemployment benefits, the single payer health program (socialized medicine originally called Obamacare), unlimited, unfettered, immigration, free public housing, and free cell phones. All of these things seem to be in league with the Bible as far as Robert is concerned. And it doesn't matter to him that the socialists champion these very same programs; after all, he thinks that the Bible proclaims a more or less socialist doctrine.

His name is Richard Black. He is a Christian, a Roman Catholic as well. Told by the Bible to feed the hungry, aid the sick, visit the imprisoned, shelter the poor, and clothe those who have no good clothes, he set out to do those very things. When it comes to voting Richard always votes Republican because he has always believed that Republicans are of the mind to follow those same Christian tenants (even though many of them aren't religious). Unlike Robert White, Richard Black subscribes to the notion that the federal government has no right to take money from the rich in order to give it to the poor. However, he, like Robert White, subscribes to the same idea that anyone who cannot take care of himself/herself has the right to expect the federal government to help them in whatever way they need to be helped—as he believes the wealthy should help the truly poor.

Because of these notions, Richard Black also backs a significant number of government programs such as giving food stamps to those who truly need life sustaining food, Social Security, Medicare, Medicaid, *limited* unemployment benefits, a fair path to citizenship, a lunch program for needy children, and a system which provides homeless shelters, for the indigent. All of these things seem to be in league with the Bible as far as Richard Black is concerned. And Richard is thankful that the majority of Republicans champion the very same programs; after all, the Bible said, "If you do these things to the least of my brothers, you will have done them to me."

The difference between these two individuals is the method they want to use to reach the very same goals.

Robert White's cohorts want the federal government to take from those who have a measure of wealth in order to give that money to those whom the government deems worthy of receiving it—including a large number of people who are not poor. This method does work. And it will work for a number of years—until those who once had money (working people, entrepreneurs, etc.) eventually go broke, at which time everyone, including the government, will be bankrupt. At that time everyone will be in the same boat: indigent. And they will be well primed to be taken over by a strong enemy.

As opposed to Robert White, Richard Black's cohorts want the federal government to take an equal percentage of money from everyone, and then distribute that money to those who need it, along with paying for all the bills the Federal government incurs. Richard says that (let's say) taking five percent from a person who makes twenty thousand dollars a year will equal two thousand dollars in taxes per year. A person who makes one million dollars per year would have to pay the government fifty thousand dollars per year (at five percent). Added together, Richard Black's method would collect way more money in taxes per year than Robert White's method. Richard says that this can be proven because, as it is now, forty to fifty percent of the population pays no tax whatsoever, even though many people in that no-pay-category make thousands of dollars per year. But this does not show because many of those people have deductions which put them below the level where taxes are required.

Richard Black maintains that his system is one that will never go broke because the taxes his tax system collects comes from the entire working (earning) population. In terms of the Bible, Richard says that nowhere does it say *how* its tenants are to be accomplished. He says it doesn't even hint that socialism is the way money should be collected and distributed. It only says what should be done to follow the Christian way. Which method is best in your mind?

I'll See You In My Dreams

When day turns into night and my head sinks into my pillow, I feel your body next to me, rising and falling in perfect rhythm. You are so calm, so content, as you slumber on through the night. As my eyes become accustomed to the dark, I turn and gaze upon the outline of your naked body: a pale white statue, with your golden hair flowing across your face, now partially hidden by your pillow. And as I worship you I think back to the beautiful girl who was once so very much in love with . . . with me.

I know your eyes will not open; I know you will not turn to offer me your arms; I know that our lips will not meet in the passion of a starry night's blissful kiss. And I know that my yearning body will remain . . . yearning. And then my mind will wander back to those warm sweet days and nights when the sparkle of anticipation would shine in your eyes and the smell of your perfume would grow stronger as you moved closer to press your soft body next to mine.

And then . . . and then . . . you stir, and you slowly turn your face to the wall that was once behind you, and I know it is time, once again, for me to whisper to you the words of a very sad song, the same words that I have whispered to you in the chilling darkness of the night for . . . for a very long time: "I'll see you in my dreams; hold you in my dreams . . . ."

Michael Blade

And when my dreams finally come, I know that you will be there at my side, and you will offer me your arms, and our lips will meet in the passion of yet another wondrous night's first kiss, and it will seem so real, and I will need to yearn for you no more because, once again, in my dreams, you will be mine.

The song, below, "I'll See You In My Dreams," was written by Isham Jones, the lyrics by Gus Kahn: May you someday hear the words and the melody of that song played as one.

"Though the days are long, twilight sings a song; a song of happiness that used to be.

Soon my eyes will close; soon I'll find repose. And in dreams you are always near me . . .

I'll see you in my dreams; hold you in my dreams, something took you out of my arms; still I feel the thrill of your charms.

Lips that once were mine, tender eyes that shine, they will light my way tonight; I'll see you in my dreams."

Until then my love. Good night.

142

Inside Out

{I once wrote a song for a famous female singer. When all was said and done she decided that because she was also a songwriter she would forever refrain from singing a new song written by someone else—meaning both the melody and the lyrics needed to be hers alone. I understood what she was saying and the melody and lyrics have been on my shelf for years. I have written music for a number of other people, but I have not offered this song—or the lyrics—to anyone until now. I would guess that these lyrics will never see the light of day as a published song. That is why I am including them in this book. These are not the greatest lyrics ever written, but they did come from my heart at the time. Maybe someone will write a melody to accompany these words. I'd like to hear it. I hope a few of you will appreciate the meaning of the words I wrote way back when.}

INSIDE OUT

The inner you, the inner me,
It's not what people seem to see;
The outer you, your mask in place,
So no one sees that hidden face.

The outer me, my fortress high,
I shed the tears that line my eyes.
So come to my garden and dance here awhile;
You'll give me your rainbow, your sun, and your smile.
And I'll give you my armor that shields you from me;
I'll sing all your praises to heaven and thee.
The inner you, the inner me, will
now be all that people see.
The outer you, the outer me, forever gone, forever free.

So, come to my garden and dance here awhile;
I'll give you my rainbow, my sun, and my smile.
The inner you, the inner me, will
now be all that people see.
The outer you, the outer me, forever gone, forever free.

Prejudice

I have touched on this subject in several of my rantings, but things still need to be said about this undying issue. Not giving a damn about political correctness, I'll ask you to suffer through this ranting as I attempt to educate some of you—in terms of the historic background involved—to the condition the entire nation (it seems) is forever debating: racial prejudice.

Before the African Negro arrived here, prejudice abounded. Prejudice against various Europeans by other Europeans. Prejudice against certain breeds of white people by other breeds of white people. Prejudice against Protestants by Catholics, prejudice against Catholics by Protestants, prejudice against certain brands of Protestantism by other brands of Protestantism. There was prejudice against Indians by non Indians, prejudice against various tribes of Indians by other tribes of Indians. Prejudice against white people by Indians. Prejudice against Indians by white people. Prejudice against Spaniards by non Spaniards, prejudice against white people by Spaniards, prejudice against Indians by Spaniards.

As some of you might guess this list is endless. But it's important for you to remember that white people did not, and still do not, hold the corner on prejudice. Prejudice abounds (rightfully or wrongfully) among every breed of people in this world (NOT JUST AMONG PEOPLE IN

THE UNITED STATES), and that includes every country that exists, or has ever existed. So, don't act as though you, or your kind, are the exception to this because if you think about it long enough, and you are honest about it, you'll come up with something or someone you are prejudice against.

[At this point it may be helpful to note Webster's definition of the word, prejudice: "An opinion, especially an unfavorable one, formed beforehand or without knowledge or thought. An unreasonable hostile attitude regarding a racial, religious, or national group. Damage or injury."]

The two key words here are "unfavorable" and "unreasonable." The word "unfavorable" bears the most weight. If a prejudicial opinion is unfavorable, then there is little basis to prove the validity of that prejudicial opinion. But if the opinion stated about a person or a thing is "unreasonable," it may still be termed prejudice, but it doesn't *necessarily* make that opinion untrue. In other words, if one asserts an unfavorable opinion about someone or something without knowledge or thought, then that person simply likes to hear himself or herself talk, and you would be foolish to pay much attention to what he or she said. Or, you can just call them prejudice and walk away. However, if they have/had knowledge of a subject, or if they have/had thought a great deal about their opinion on a subject, then calling them prejudice may have just as much to do with your own personal prejudices as it does with what you presume to be their personal prejudices.

As you have seen, prejudice against one another didn't begin with black people and it won't end with them. But anti-black prejudice is all anyone seems to want to talk about these days, so it might be more relevant to you were I to address that narrow subject rather than to speak in generalities about all the other races in this pitiful world. (Be aware that I could have selected any other race, religion, or creed, and the story would end up being similar when it came to views of prejudice about/against those entities.)

A bit of history:

Black Africans were more than happy to remain in Africa before, during, and after Columbus (or whoever) founded the New World. When it eventually became necessary to acquire cheap labor, indentured laborers (slaves in effect) from a host of geographical areas in the world were brought to the colonies. In the beginning the vast majority of these laborers were white; they were not African negroes. Eventually, white ship owners chummed up with other ship owners (including Arab traders) and the "triangle" was born. This triangle consisted of the trade of sugar/ molasses, tobacco, and human slaves (and later wheat and rum). The triangle itself involved the Caribbean Islands and later America, Africa, and Europe (mainly England).

Eventually, more and more manpower was needed to do the work the land owners and business owners needed to have done in order to carry on their businesses and grow in wealth. Unfortunately for the black Africans, the cheapest manpower could be found within their continent. In short, land and business owners found it less trying on their pocketbooks—as well as their consciences—to acquire humans that were less like them. And the black natives of Africa seemed to fit that bill quite nicely as far as they were concerned.

Knowing that many of these black Africans tended to sup upon one another, that they were wont to place bones through the lower part of their noses, stretch their ears and lips, causing them to look frighteningly different from the run of the mill white immigrant, it seemed to be a natural thing for the colonists to purchase these "semi-humans" to do the work they neither wanted to do, nor were capable of doing in order to become successful entrepreneurs.

Both the intelligence level and the civility of those black people brought here seemed to be way below the norm as far as the white people were concerned. In other words, they were not seen as equals to the "civilized" people living here. Stated even more bluntly— "civilized" people were not about to treat these black heathens as equals. (This had to be said despite your feelings of indignation as you sit here reading this so many years later.) The notion that African negroes were people too, and that they had souls just like other people, was something that few slave owners took into account back then—probably because most of these people did their best to block that notion from their consciences. Had they not been able to do so, history would not have gone down the way it did. What's more, various Protestant sects made up their own Christian value systems, and many of those systems allowed for slavery.

In light of the above, and knowing that a vast difference existed between the dominant (white) race already established here, and the black heathen newcomers, it seemed natural for most of the "civilized" people here to look upon these "natives" as being in a category that ranged from "pet" status all the way up the latter to the sub-human dimwit level. (Mankind can be so wonderful at times, can't it?)

I suppose that certain blacks reading these words are fuming by now. But cut the fuming; you know damn well that had the roles been reversed, the black aristocratic majority living here back then would have treated the whites in exactly the same manner. In other words, certain inclinations mankind seems to have are really fucked up! You know what I'm sayin'?

As time passed it became apparent that some of these black African slaves weren't as stupid as it was once thought. Some of them were actually smart, some were quite handsome (beautiful), and some were even more adept at doing certain things than some of their lazy ass white owners. It even got to the point where the slaves were raising their owner's white children better than the white slave owners were capable of doing. "Holy shit!" I'm sure some of these white slave owners were saying to themselves. "Someday we might have to admit that these slaves are actually . . . actually . . . human!"

Slowly, the tide began to turn. Soon half the population of this country realized that these black slaves were indeed human, that they had souls, that they had feelings, and that they wanted to become civilized and live their lives just like their white counterparts. Many white slave owners began to give up their slaves by freeing them. However, many other slave owners did not share that attitude. This was so, in large part, because their well being depended on cheap labor. In short, they could not admit that the blacks were in any way equal to them. If they did they would have to set them free. (Look up the Dred Scott case.)

A fiercely debated question arose: Did the Constitution say, and mean, that all men are created equal in every way? Or did it say, and mean, that all men are created equal UNDER THE LAW? Or, did it say both positions were/ are equally true? Last, did it say that none of those postures were true?

Actually, the Constitution's stand was this: God created all men equal in terms of their souls and their right to exist on this planet as free people. But the Constitution did not imply that all men were created equal in terms of their capabilities, or their appearance, or their individual talents.

Lincoln and his Republicans won the day: All men were created equal under the law. That meant slavery was not only evil, but that it was also unconstitutional. A war ensued and the slaves were freed. But this didn't quell the hostilities that existed among certain white men, and certain other white men and their black "counterparts." The majority of blacks still looked sub-human to many white people. These white people thought that because a group of people had been proclaimed equal under the law it did not mean that they were equal in appearance, intellectual capabilities, or in their mannerisms when compared to their white counterparts living here.

Nevertheless, the slow process began of the education and enculturation of the former black slaves. Over the years blacks have become great in every aspect of life in this country, including intellectual endeavors, business, sports, religion, entertainment, politics, and the list goes on. Unfortunately, however, the antics of a minority of blacks living in this country tend to overshadow the goodness of the black majority. That problem needs to be addressed.

Unfortunately, or fortunately (depending how you look at it) the majority of blacks in this country are identifiable. Blacks don't like this identity factor, and they will say that they are still selected against for no other reason than their skin color. But I say," bullshit!" Have you ever heard of the expression, "Actions speak louder than words?"

Guess what: actions speak louder than skin color as well. Like it or not, a racial minority is always identifiable in a culture of people not of that same racial or cultural background. You think a white person walking around in a city located in the heart of Africa is not going to stand out! Think again.

So, when one black person does something wrong, not much is said about it other than maybe, "That's life." But when a pattern emerges like the so called "knock-out punch" bullshit, which, at its emergence, was conducted exclusively by blacks, then blacks, in total, suffer. Do you think it was any different when the Irish came here drinking and brawling? Same when boatloads of Jews came here. How about the Chinese who worked on the railroads? Germans during the two World Wars? Japanese during the World War II? It may not be morally justified, but prejudices against minorities will be the rule every time noticeable numbers of people from those minorities do things that either distress or infuriate the majority.

People like Oprah Winfrey can proclaim all she wants that such reactions will wither away once the present day older generation finally dies out, but she has no idea what the hell she's talking about. Here's what's real, Winfrey: As long as certain races and/or breeds of people can be identified as being apart from the majority (because of how they act, or what they do) then those people will be selected against, particularly when groups from those minorities do things to infuriate the majority. So, you can insult the older generation in this country all you want, Winfrey, because it still happens to be a free country, but know this: prejudice knows no age, and it exists in every race. As I said, you can wish away the older generation, but those who come after them (the new older generation) will have prejudices as well. And that includes prejudice black people. How many generations have to die in your mind before you realize that?

The only thing that will prevent the negative sort of unfounded prejudice discussed in the first part of this rant is when minorities become mirror images of the majority. What I mean is this: no matter how black, yellow, or brown one's skin is, if a person of "color" living in this society dresses, talks, acts, and thinks like the majority, he/she will be accepted as being a part of that majority. At that point, if a majority white person treats a minority person in a true prejudicial manner, then that white person should be made to suffer the consequences. How about banishing him/her to live out their sentence in an African country where they will quickly learn the meaning of (reverse) prejudice!

The surest way for black people (as well as other minorities) to overcome prejudice in this country is to convince their youth to attend and do well in school, to quit having babies out of wedlock, to build cohesive families with the male as the family's leader, to live within the law, and to basically act like everyone else in terms of dress, speech and civility.

By the way, those things go for the white majority as well.

Be Thankful For

Being able to complain about your government because it means you have freedom of speech.

Your heating and electric bills because they make your house warm and well lit.

Your laundry that needs cleaning because it means you can afford to own clothes.

Your dry throat and wrinkled face in the morning because it means that you're alive to live another day.

The noisy kids next door because it means that you can still hear, and that the human race will continue.

Being a little overweight because it means that you are not starving.

The house you have to clean for your upcoming party because it means that people care enough about you to come to your house.

The taxes you have to pay because it means you have income.

Your spouse who gets into bed when you do because you know he/she will not be out sleeping with someone else.

The house chores you continually have to do because it means you have a place to live.

Your car maintenance bill because it means you have a car to drive.

The ticket you got because it reminds you that there are people out there trying to prevent you and others from getting killed.

Your faith because it reminds you that this life is not all there is.

And there is so much more.

Going To College

Despite what your parents (and practically the whole world) have told you—not all high school graduates need to/should go to college. That includes your kid! In short, the main reason a person would need to go to college is to take the classes one needs to take to enable one to pursue a specific career. You need to go to college to become a doctor, a teacher, a lawyer, and a host of other professions requiring what is termed a "higher education." So, if that's the case, fine, go to college. But the majority of jobs in these fifty states do not require a college degree. What is needed is skill and the ability to learn (and do) the job required of a given worker. And guess what? Many of these non-college jobs pay more than a college graduate is able to earn in the prestigious profession he or she is able to find.

They'll throw statistics at you indicating that in the long run college graduates will earn more money than non graduates, but I say it ain't always so in light of the fact that a huge number of college graduates constantly move from job to job, trying to move up in the world, but in the process they often lose many of the benefits they would have accrued had they stayed where they were. But when, say, a plumber moves to a new company he can more or less maintain a plumber's salary. What's more, he can take his

401K with him, and he doesn't have to start all over again learning how to do his (or her) job.

Even if the average college graduate has the ability to earn more money over his or her lifetime, I say, so freaking what! Those statistics don't imply that a college graduate is happier than a non-college graduate during his or her lifetime. What's more, you have to get it through your head that some kids are simply not meant to go to college. You can pay tons of money to have your son or daughter go to college, only to find that your $90K can't/didn't/won't help him or her find that fabulous career you both expected him or her to find. And there is nothing more discouraging to a person than it is for them to find that their expectations will never be met.

I have a number of children. Half of them went to college and are very successful in their professions. They indeed love what they do. The other half did not go to college. The ones that did not go to college have all made millions, and they all love what they do as well.

As a father I did not tell any of my children to go to college. Fact is I used myself as an example: I sold pharmaceuticals and taught school. College was necessary to get those jobs. However, I made my living (almost my entire life) in an industry that did not require one day of college. Simply stated, as it turned out, I could not have made the money I made had I stayed in any of the professions I chose requiring a college degree.

Take a moment to analyze your thoughts. Do you want all of your children to go to college because you simply think it's the thing to do? Is it because you will feel shame if they don't go? Will they feel shame if they don't go, just because that is what is expected of them?

Maybe one of your kids loves to cook. Would either of you be ashamed if he or she went to a school that taught him or her how to be a chef? Many chefs make a ton of money! And the ones I know love what they do. Do I need to list all the occupations that don't require a college education that can make a person rich? And don't forget that it is always possible for a son or daughter to go into a trade and wind up going into that same business for themselves. The bottom line to all of this is to find a line of work that you love, a line that makes you feel as though you are accomplishing the things you are interested in accomplishing. If you can do that without having to go to college, then great! If you can't, then by all means go to college. It's just that simple.

And don't let anyone feed you that bullshit line about not being "well-rounded" if you don't go to college. My father didn't go past the 5th grade. He not only became a wealthy entrepreneur, but he was also one of the most well read guys I have ever known.

One more thing: I believe that every college in this country should be obligated to have a trade school attached to it. Not every college would be able to offer every trade. Each college could offer a different set of specialized trades. Your child could then choose to go to the college that offered the trade he or she wanted to learn.

Best of all, both the time and money spent attaining the expertise a student would need to get a job in his or her chosen field, would be far less than the usual thousands almost every college charges their students to get their degree in a field in which they will most likely never work.

What's more, if I had anything to say about it I would compel the trade school student to complete three classes with a minimum grade of "C" in order to earn his or her trade certificate: A basic math class, a basic English class, and a basic United States history class.

Read this "ranting" with your son or daughter. Maybe it will help you decide the best course of action to take.

College Professors

I got okay grades in grammar school. I got into trouble a lot; I was good in sports, sang in the choir, played several musical instruments, and I had an easy time with girls. High school was no different except for the fact that although I was still good at most sports, I was doomed not to participate in those endeavors because my hair was too long to suit the fancy of my dumb-ass high school coaches. Because I refused to assume the role of a "jock" by cutting my quaff to the point of baldness, the coaches got together and banned me from playing any sport until I decided to acquiesce. I did not acquiesce.

My reaction to all of this was to tell all the coaches to kiss my young ass, which further alienated me from those fine fellows. Thus it was my high school teams never had a winning season while I was there—which, of course, I attributed to the fact that I was not allowed to play. That does have a ring of truth to it by the way.

Managing to attain for myself a GPA of 1.8, I graduated from high school, without honors, and soon found myself headed for a career as a packager in a cookie jar plant. Fuck that! Two weeks later I joined the U.S. Naval Reserves, and on the following day I registered as a freshman at a nearby junior college. Multiple parental heart attacks ensued.

Being with people who didn't have to be where they were, I suddenly turned an about face and I actually became interested in learning about things such as government, politics, history, economics, and business, along with a few other topics such as geology and paleontology.

Upon transferring to a four year college, I eventually found myself earning a 3.8 grade point average. I also found that the majority of my college professors were quite liberal in terms of the way they slanted their lectures. Let me rephrase that. Almost to the man (or woman) they were a bunch of fucking anti-American socialist idiots!

I was a bit older than most of the other students in my classes. Three years at the most. But those three years were like three hundred years in terms of the differences that existed between the way they thought and the way I thought. The 1960's were at their height. So was the Viet Nam war. And I couldn't believe the differences that existed between the majority of the students and me in terms of our mutual thoughts about the war, about this country, about the "American way," and about drugs.

I quickly became "the opposing side" whenever it came to presenting an opposing opinion to whatever the professor had said. One time, after finishing a verbal report to the class on the geopolitics of Italy (in which I happened to mention that one could not be, in all conscience, a practicing Catholic and a staunch communist AT THE SAME TIME), the Student Body President of the school (who happened to be in my class) stormed out of the room, but not before first saying that I was full of shit, and that it was certainly philosophically possible for a practicing Christian/Catholic to be a practicing communist at the same time! In other words, he was saying that it is philosophically possible to be a practicing Christian and an atheist at the same time. What a freaking moron! After class several people came up to me and quietly told me that they agreed with what I had said. In all the classes I had (I graduated with over 600 units) not one of my professors could be termed "middle-of-the-road," let alone one of them espousing a philosophy to the right of center.

What caused this phenomenon? I don't have enough energy to go into it. (Remember, I'm old.) All I will say is that back then somewhere in the neighborhood of ninety per cent of all college professors teaching government, political science, economics, and/or history, taught their classes from a liberal to socialist viewpoint. And that is still the case today. This means that all your charming little children are learning to be loyal anti-American socialists, all of whom will graduate and then walk around with blinders on their eyes to the realities of life, totally incapable of seeing the truth in anything other than what they have been taught to see by their liberal/socialist teachers. And you wonder why this country is so screwed up!

I should add that the students who are capable of seeing what I am saying are perpetually forced to regurgitate the socialist line back to their professors in the reports they are assigned to write, because if they don't they'll get a bad grade. And if that happens they will be screwing themselves because those grades will be seen on the resumes they will be forced to show their potential employers.

This practice of hiring only leftist college professors is almost impossible to brake. This will remain so no matter who is president, or who controls the Congress. It will take generations to change this condition, if it can be done at all. In the interim it will be up to you to teach your children the value of being presented both sides of a given issue in their liberal arts classes and on the television channels they watch.

You may recall my saying that this country will eventually fall because of socialism (among other things), but you, as parents, can at least delay that inevitable reality by seeing to it that your children learn the value of a fair and balanced education.

On the other hand, you are most likely the product of that socialist education and will be opposed to almost everything I have said. Let's face it, your kids are screwed. And their kids as well, and their kids, and . . . .

Wings

Chances are you are the product of our education system. When I say "you" I'm talking about those of you who were subjected to the slanted philosophies of those in charge of our educational system ever since the early 1960's.

Topics such as math, general science, English, foreign languages, medicine, and agriculture have been, and still are, taught in a fairly straight forward manner without too much bullshit thrown into the mix. Philosophies within these subjects exist, but they are minor when compared to those contained within the Arts, particularly political science, government and economics.

Running through almost every one of these subjects is a philosophy that can be structuralized and shown on various charts. Right wing, left wing, conservative, liberal, radical, progressive, communist, fascist, libertarian, populist, anarchist, are some of the philosophies categorized and listed on these charts which are studied by students in college classes, and even before that in their high school classes.

Instead of constructing these charts in a manner that would be perfectly understandable to a student with an IQ of 65, those in power chose (and still choose) to misrepresent the positions they list on their charts. They did this, and still do this, in order to convince their students that their philosophy (the teachers) was/is one that could/can be seen as being the standard when it came/comes to the proper categorization of the political philosophies they are discussing.

Case in point:

Political philosophies, when placed on a chart, would make the most sense were they to range from Communism and Fascism (both requiring total government control) to anarchy, which is the total lack of government—meaning no control of any sort. A chart like this would appear as follows:

Communism and Fascism, Autocracy (religious or otherwise), Democracy, Constitutional Federal Republic, Libertarian, Anarchy.

A more intricate chart would range from certain nonreligious dictatorships, to Islamic types of dictatorships run by Imams and the like, to the semi-dictatorial rule of kings and queens, to strict majority rule democracies, to democracies whose representatives are elected by the people, but can be overruled by a central government (that's the USA today), to a democratic form of government with representatives who congregate in a central place, whereupon they supposedly relate the wishes of those who elected them to the total representative body, all of which is subject to certain checks and balances. (That is the government our founding fathers hoped Americans would adopt and maintain: a constitutional federal republic.) After that we move to a libertarian form of government with almost no governmental restrictions on the electorate of any kind, to anarchy with no government whatsoever (which would automatically lead to chaos and the rule of the mighty, and would, of course, eventually lead us, full circle, right back to totalitarianism).

As you can see, this chart ranges from total government control, to no government at all. But guess what the cagy educators in charge of our esteemed educational system decided to do. They decided to stick fascism on the right side of the chart (spectrum) after a constitutional federal republic, somewhere between libertarianism and anarchy. This made it easy for left wing historians, sociologists, economists, and others to make their case against what they called/call the fanatic, radical, uncaring, greedy right. To make it easy for these "educators" to get their points across to their simpleminded students, they slyly created a political party chart for each of our major political parties; it ended up looking like this:

The Democratic Party: Far left/ Liberal/Middle of the road.

The Republican Party: Middle of the road/Conservative/ Fascist.

Notice the absence of a Communist category on the left. Instead, it is merely called "the far left." Notice the inclusion of Fascism on the right. Were I to look at the above chart, I would conclude that, yes, the Democratic Party has its leftist members, but most of its members are liberals, or middle of the road Democrats, and a few of its members might even vote for a conservative position or two; but all and all its members are a pretty damn nice group of people, only interested in helping the struggling middle class and the poor. How quaint.

Of the members of the Republican Party, I would conclude that there are a few middle-of-the-roaders, but basically that party consists of a bunch of narrow minded conservatives, with a large number of radicals in control, and at the extreme, fascists, interested only in waging war on foreign countries in order to gain ever increasing power over every other nation in the world. Knowing that there are fascists on this chart, I would conclude that if they could these Republicans would eradicate every race, every color, and every philosophy, other than their own, and by so doing create a fascist state (and world) once only dreamed of by their right wing hero, Adolph Hitler.

A bit of a stretch for any logical person to swallow. But that's what our wonderful college professors want their students to take away from their classes. Of course, don't expect them to admit it.

It goes without saying that this spectrum being taught by our professors is pure bullshit! In other words, it's time for students to reprogram their brains to recognize the political spectrum as it really exists.

For the record it is important to note that people can be political liberals yet be economic conservatives. And the opposite can also be true—people can be political conservatives, yet be economic liberals, although the latter is not a common position.

However, for our purposes, it's easier to speak in more general terms than it is to list every little exception that might arise. For example, a political liberal championing abortion, huge government spending programs, excess welfare, etc., can still be for certain laissez faire economic policies. Conversely, a conservative also can be for abortion, opposed to excessive welfare programs, but a champion of massive government spending in other areas. But that sort of conservative would be the exception.

It is also important for you to know the difference between communism and fascism. Communism is a political system where the government owns everything and then parcels out its goods and services to whomever it wishes. It owns every business and everything used to operate that business; it also owns everything that a business creates and sells—with very few exceptions. With this form of government, a small group of people rule over everything and everyone. The leader in a communist country is a dictator in as much as the cadre of people ruling with him allow him to be so. This is totalitarianism at its best. Remember, the communist mantra (adopted from Carl Marx) is: "From each according to his ability, to each according to his needs." In other words, you make as much as you possibly can, and I will take whatever I want from you, and I will give it to whomever I think needs it." Is that system up your alley? Are you sure?

With fascism, the government, controlled by its dictator, may or may not technically own everything (businesses, land, etc.), as with communism, but one way or another it has absolute control over all of those things. In short, the dictator controlling a fascist country controls everything and everyone in that country (as did Hitler), and the people have no say in their government whatsoever. You can see why both communism and fascism belong beside one another as they are both totalitarian systems. That is why the participants of these two systems

(Germany and Russia) hated one another so much while they were vying for power during the 1930's and 1940's.

Last, I hope that by now you have noticed that socialism was not listed as a political system. That's because it is not a political system. It is, instead, an economic system. A government utilizing this economic system controls the economy without actually owning the businesses it controls. (A bit fascist wouldn't you say?) In effect, it dictates to business owners how, what, where, and when things are to be produced and sold. This system strives to control every aspect of a country's economy. By so doing the everyday life of the people living under that system is affected. Socialist rule seeks to take from those it deems to have too much, in order to give to those it deems to be lacking in whatever the government says they are lacking. Think of Obamacare and the offshoot it has created. It is socialism at its worst, and once it takes full control it will effectively destroy our once fabulous healthcare system, and from there—our nation. Do you see how communism, fascism, and the economic system, socialism, seem to flow together?

Unfortunately, many countries in the world use a number of variations of this economic system to steer their economies—all without success. (I've already explained the few exceptions to this.)

The next time you see a chart showing a political spectrum, especially our country's political spectrum, don't just accept what you see. Question your teacher's or your professor's positions; question also the textbooks you are forced to "learn" from as being the up-to-date truth in terms of the subject you are "learning." It will be interesting to watch those teachers spin their way around your questions.

In the end you can even regurgitate their teachings back to them in the papers you are assigned to write. But, in your own mind you will know that there is another side to the so-called truth they have dished out to you.

China

As of this writing China's destiny is to control the world; and it *will* do so barring certain radical changes in the way the United States and its leaders do things. But those changes are not in the cards. As things are now, China's economy is expanding exponentially. Soon, her economy will dwarf America's dying economy and she will dictate to every nation on earth how things must be done—or else! And don't fall for the BS the press tries to tell you about China's economy being on the brink of collapse. They simply have growing pains. The Chinese can falter here and there but they are making so much money it's almost impossible for that country to go down for the count.

Look at almost everything you buy and you will see the label, "Made in China" on it. "Yes, but I only buy American," you say. Yeah, right. And you'll pay nearly twice as much for whatever you buy. And even if you were to hold that position, you'll eventually brake down and buy the Chinese item because, after all, you're not stupid! And eventually you'll think that it's okay to buy Chinese because it doesn't really hurt our country in the long run— "Because we're Americans!" Note: Bullshit! It does hurt our country when you buy foreign products—especially products from China that could be made here.

As in many of these articles, I can't take the time to write hundreds of pages trying to prove what I'm telling you. You most likely wouldn't read those pages anyway. It is in that light that I will attempt to summarize what the problem is, and then I'll give some suggestions regarding how this problem can be resolved.

Because of the thinking of every one of our presidents, from Obama clear back to Nixon, our economy has been slowly falling apart. A major reason for this is because those people thought/think it would be wise to do business with China. Why? Because it appeared to them as though we would benefit from this so-called "mutual business enterprise." We would make our products, ship them over to China, and make billions because we would be exposed to a huge population wildly thirsting for all of our wonderful products. In return, we would buy certain products from the Chinese, products we really didn't/don't care to manufacture in our country. (You know, like all the dumb-ass cheap stuff the Japanese made trying to get on their feet after WWII.)

The mutual trade agreements we agreed upon were supposed to benefit both countries. Those Presidents mentioned did their best to convince the American public that these "agreements" would be fabulous for our country, and would, in turn, take us a long way toward "normal" relations with our (one time?) enemy, China.

But it didn't quite work out to our advantage. Take into consideration the following: 1) China is a communist country; it can make its people do anything it wants them to do, 2) the Chinese pay their laborers a disgracefully low wage, 3) because of this the Chinese can afford to offer their products at a considerable discount when compared to the same price for the same products made in the U.S.,

4) the Chinese levy tariffs on our products when they enter their country, and 5) the Chinese don't give a shit if their products are inferior, or are dangerous to the people who buy them. Thus, the U.S. and its greedy entrepreneurs (in conjunction with certain Wall Street fat cats) rushed to the table to create the laws necessary to allow those trade agreements to go into effect. And the citizens of this country got screwed in the process.

Why did we get screwed? Because instead of this agreement becoming mutually beneficial to both countries, it has turned into a one-sided route by China over the U.S. Why? Because China has been able to undercut our prices with almost every one of their products. Why the hell would you buy a television made in the U.S. for $2,800.00, when you could buy an equal television made in China and sold here for $1300.00?

American union leaders forever cry and moan about Americans who do not buy products made in America. But hay, you know what Union leaders—you have driven up the cost of American made products because of the inordinately high wages you have gleaned from our business owners here; so high that our business owners can no longer afford to make their products at a competitive price when compared to the prices China is able to charge. What the hell do you expect people to do—buy products just because they are union made, and pay twice the amount for those products in the process? Get real. Hey, it's real nice that your unions got our American businesses to pay inordinately high wages and benefits to your members, but you are killing those businesses in the process because many of our businesses can no longer make a profit. So, they go out of business and guess what—your union members find themselves out of a job.

Another reason why American businesses are failing (or can't even get off the ground) is because of all the idiotic laws and stipulations business owners have to endure if they want to conduct their businesses here.

I know how to make the best peanut brittle in the history of the world; its flavor is like nothing you have ever tasted; and it doesn't stick to your teeth. I tried to go into business some years back, but it was next to impossible for me to do so. I had very little money back then and nobody I knew thought peanut brittle was worth investing in. In addition to that there were so many laws and stipulations and added expenses that I would have been forced to deal with that my chances of success were practically nil.

Had I been able to pull it off at the time I probably would have become a multi-millionaire. I know people would have gone nuts over my peanut brittle (no pun intended). But, I had no chance. I would have to have been a millionaire to afford the cost of going into that crummy little business. So, I had to say, "Hell with it; let them eat the sticky crap they have always eaten." I still have the secret recipe; I make it every Christmas. And if I don't package a ton of it for my family and friends each year, everyone gets all pissed at me.

Time to take a real educated guess: do you think the Chinese (at this writing) have to go through the same shit (that I would have been forced to go through) to make their products? Of course they don't. They don't have to go through any of it. And that's another reason why they can undercut our prices. It's quite simple really.

As a result of this catastrophic situation, America's businesses are moving to China (in droves) in order to cash in on their cheap labor force. You would die if you knew how many American businesses are moving there, or have already moved there: Coka-Cola, Caterpillar, and GE just to name three major companies. (Go to jiesworld.com for a more complete list.) In other words, many of the products made by these companies are now made by Chinese workers, in China, instead of American workers here in the U.S.! Are you surprised? Doesn't it just thrill you to know these things? Then again, maybe you don't care about it in the least.

So, hay, it's either stay in America and go out of business, or move to China and continue making millions. It's just that simple. The only thing is literally thousands of Americans have lost, are losing, and will lose their jobs here as a result of this pathetic situation. And the politicians and the unions here are too fucking stupid and/or gutless (take your choice) to do anything about it.

That's why I say that China will one day rule the world. All they have to do is break us first. And who is going to stop that from happening—you? Don't you just love the way our unions and our burgeoning socialist government does things? The irony is that China, a communist country, is screwing us by using, as its economic model, our own dying capitalist system—minus the slave labor factor long ago abandoned in our country.

Go Socialism!

Sex: Midlife Through Old Age

Yeah, right!

(Okay, you know what? I was going to leave this page blank after the above, "*Yeah right!*" It was intended to be a sarcastic statement. Instead, as sort of a bonus, I am going to enlighten you men about a very small part of your sex life that I'm guessing you probably have never contemplated.)

Men: Have you ever wondered why so many of YOU (men) have suffered from premature ejaculation throughout your adult lives? The reason for this malady is really quite simple: It is because since the age of eight (or less) you have most likely masturbated somewhere in the neighborhood of 4,320 times (give or take three times, and assuming that you are now about thirty years of age).

Now follow this: The goal of masturbation is to reach a climax as quickly as possible. Unfortunately, however, your body/brain can't tell the difference between a climax due to masturbation, and one resulting from the act of sexual intercourse. Thus, as it is with your two to three minutes of masturbation, it now takes you a mere two to three minutes to reach a climax with your sexual partner.

But, unfortunately for you, you can bet that your partner isn't too fond of this situation. As a matter of fact, at this juncture she may be secretly thrilled to get it over with (each time) because she knows that she's not even going to come close to having a climax of her own! Indeed, she's probably resolved to the fact that she'll be lucky if she manages to have a maximum of two orgasms a year with those two to three minutes you so generously allot her whenever the two of you have sex. Of course, she also knows that even that won't happen if you don't first engage in a ton of foreplay. And so she continues on with her fake groaning (or however she handles it), and you have your climax and then quickly head for sleep thinking all the while that your woman is indeed lucky to have you for a sexual partner.

I'll tell you what—you damn well better give your woman a whole lot of credit for putting up with that shit for as long as she has. It's only because she loves you that she tolerates your sexual inadequacies. And it is for that same reason that she may not even mention that there is a problem in the first place.

There is a remedy for this problem, but I'm not going to go into it. Look it up yourself if you think it may be important in terms of the wellbeing of your relationship. And by the way, you might think about finding a way to inform your sons about this problem. I'm not saying it necessarily should come from you, but you would do well for them if you found a way.

So Many Things

There are so many things I would like to tell you before I write the words, THE END. But I won't be able to do so because it would take too many pages. Like vitamins. I'd love to tell you what vitamins the average person should take at certain ages. But I won't because I don't want to hear all the stupid remarks people would make about what I would tell (you) them. "How do you know what people should take, you're not a doctor." "What might work for one person might not work for another person," and so on. Yeah, right; brilliant! So, hell with it; die early.

I'd also like to tell you about some of the best prescription drugs to take for certain ailments, but I won't for the same reasons stated above. Did I just hear someone say, "This guy thinks he knows everything about everything." Answer: No, I don't, but I do know a little bit about certain things—like drugs and medicine—because, like I said in another "ranting," I used to work for some top notch pharmaceutical companies that manufacture many of those items. My job was to teach doctors how to prescribe our drugs to their patients so as not to kill them. But, you know what—hell with that too; go buy a Merck Manual and a PDR (Physicians Desk Reference) and read things for yourself—if you can understand what those books are telling you. Maybe you'll stumble across the answers to the questions you may have about drugs and vitamins. Of course you may also end up thinking you have every disease known to man while you're at it!

In lieu of the above, I will instead tell you what really pisses me off, or worse, what I hate. Maybe some of these things piss you off as well. Time to rant:

I hate being put on "hold" for ten minutes, and then get a fucking dial tone.

I hate rats, mice, termites, wasps, birds that shit on my car's windshield, dogs that shit on my lawn, bark all day, and/or drool.

I hate white people who hate all non white people just because they are not white people.

I hate all non white people who blame white people for just about everything bad that happens to non white people.

I hate most of the richest people in the world because they almost all try to use their wealth to rule other people, because to them their wealth is proof that they are smarter than everyone else, hence, they believe that only they know all the answers.

I hate flying in airplanes because I have to place my life in someone else's hands (among four hundred other reasons).

I hate waiting in lines because I feel it is life-time wasted.

I hate most publishing companies and publishers; I place them on par with car dealers and shyster lawyers.

I hate people who claim to be singer/songwriters and only contribute a few notes and/or words to the majority of their songs—and there are many of them who do that— and you'd be shocked if you knew who some of them were/ are. And I'm not going to tell you who they were/are.

I hate the fact that after both John Kennedy and Ronald Reagan implored me to run for a Congressional seat, I did not do so.

I hate the fact that I played on Rickey Nelson's flag football team (on the field at U.C.L.A.) instead of Elvis's team, because they kicked our ass every time we played them. (Elvis and his teammates were a bunch of crazy sum-bitches out on that field!)

I hate the fact that I failed to pursue even one of my inventions/patents to the extent that I was able to begin a business using one of them. They would have helped a lot of people. Guess I was a lousy promoter. (Is there still time? Not.)

I hate the fact that I never made an album of my songs.

I hate the fact that I have taken far more than I have given in life.

I hate bathrooms that are out of paper towels.

I hate people who don't flush after crapping in a public toilet.

I hate people who talk on their cell phones in their cars while driving.

I fucking hate the word, "misspoke."

I hate people who say, "At the end of the day," and use the words, "Slippery slope," all the time because at the end of the day slippery slopes are actually quite dangerous.

I hate hackers and identity thieves; I think they should all be strung up by their balls (ovaries).

I hate sleeping on beds that aren't Sleep Number beds. (65)

I hate not being able to eat onions and garlic anymore.

I hate seeing people go hungry, people in pain, people in morning for a loved one, an American soldier die in a useless war, countries that use poison gas on civilians, an unjust aggressor nation, incurable diseases, earthquakes because there is nowhere to hide, true racism, alcoholism, drug addiction, abortion, religious hypocrisy, religious persecution, and cruelty to animals. I hate not being able to play well all the instruments I was once able to play well, and that I am unable to sing as well as I could when I was young.

I hate the cheapened way they make candy these days (except for Sees).

I hate what legalizing marijuana is going to do to our already fucked up society.

I hate Presidents, Congressmen, and Senators who lie to the people who elected them.

I hate the people who are trying to eradicate our Constitution.

I hate cold weather.

I hate excessively hot weather.

I hate people who have children out of wedlock and then abandon them because they don't want the responsibility.

I hate it that young people have abandoned books in favor of videogames and TV sitcoms.

I hate it that people (especially young people) spend so much time playing games and sending and reading emails and texts on their stupid cell phones because it will one day prove to be one of the biggest suppressors of creativity the world will ever witness. (Ask Einstein.)

Oh yeah, and I hate people who hate everything.

Islam

I have studied Islam for a long time. I'm not talking about reading an article here and there. I'm talking about reading a host of Korans (or Qurans), meaning, "the Recital," written by different people from different "sects" within that religion. Add to that the study of a number of Hadiths (Muhammad's tradition), written by several different interpreters of that book, along with a host of other books written by members of the various sects within that religion.

This "ranting" is not meant to be a history of Islam, or the various sects within that religion. It is merely my take on what I have learned about Islam and its followers, along with a number of observations that I will make about that religion.

First, the American Muslims I personally know are very nice, sincere, fun loving, seemingly happy, honest, devoted people. Yet, even they fall into the overall category of people I will be talking about. In other words, Muslims, who adhere to the faith known as Islam, basically have the same goals the world over, because the basic literature they read insists upon their meeting those goals. In that light it may be easier for you to understand what I'll say about Islam if I lay out a bit of groundwork for you.

Let us agree that the average Christian believes that God exists, that Jesus Christ was/is His son, and that there is a heaven along with a place known as hell. Let's also agree that these Christians believe that Christ died for everyone's sins, that one's sins, after accepting Christ, are forgiven, that their future sins can be forgiven, and that the Bible is the written word of God. Let us further agree that these Christians believe that the Ten Commandments should be followed. Last, let us concur that Christians believe that they should love their fellow man, that the souls of all men are created equal in the eyes of God, that all people on earth should become Christian, and that no one should be *forced* to become a follower of Christ. Generalities? Of course. How else can you talk about these things if you can't talk in generalities? In any case, I think most Christians will agree with what I have just said.

The Shahada proclaims the basic belief of Islam. Its overall proclamation says that, "There is no God but Allah, and that Muhammad is His profit." So, Muslims definitely believe that God exists. They believe that Christ *existed* as well, but that he was little more than a prophet and had no Godlike powers. They do not believe that Christ rose from the dead after he was crucified. In fact, many Muslims do not believe that Jesus of Nazareth was even crucified, saying that it was someone else that died on the cross that day. What's more, Muslims do not believe in the virgin birth of Jesus, and they certainly don't believe that Jesus was conceived by the work of the Holy Spirit. They believe that Joseph of Nazareth was Jesus' natural father; therefore Jesus could not have been related to God in any way. After all, Mary, a human, was married to Joseph, not to God! Last, most Muslims believe in an afterlife, but that afterlife is markedly different from the Christian notion of heaven. Virgins for men, fine wines, and pleasurable comforts rank high in a Muslim's vision of the rewards of heaven. On the other hand, not much is said about what women get.

For years, most of the interpreters of the Koran ("Quran") believed that black people could not enter their Muslim heaven. (See Sura 3:106.) They have managed to cover up those teachings by explaining them away (see their theories of Abrogation and Nullification), and they get quite irritated when those teachings are mentioned—if younger Muslims even know about those teachings these days. (Read Sura 49:13 and Sura 30:22 to see the changes Muslims made in relation to Sura 3:106.) In truth, there are later utterances by Muhammad that black people are accepted as equals (see the Nullification theory).

All Muslims (meaning they who submit to Islam) are taught that the world is destined to become an Islamic world, and that it doesn't matter how that feat is accomplished, as long as it is accomplished. Thus, anything done to advance that condition is right, just, and good. This includes a carefully designed Muslim population explosion in certain countries, quickened by a multiplicity of wives (remember, many Muslim men have up to four wives). This rapid increase of the Muslim population in a given country has/will eventually enable Muslims to control the ballot boxes (especially in democratic countries) making violent takeovers unnecessary. Last, acts of violence are used to acquire the power necessary to take over a given part of a country, or the country itself. This falls under their definition of the word, "Jihad, "(which means "to struggle"). In short, militant Muslims say, "Whatever works," when it comes to their plan to rule the world, thereby making all people subject to Islam (and to them).

There are many Muslims in the world who know absolutely nothing about what I have just said. Most of these people are illiterate. They live in Muslim dominated countries, and are concerned only with staying alive, and staying alive is more often than not predicated on one's outward practice of Islam. They may pray up to five times a day (which is not a bad thing); they may even hold the Koran in their hands when they pray, but most of the Korans they hold are printed in Arabic, and a huge number of Muslims cannot even read Arabic, let alone read their own written language. Most Muslims try to do "the right thing," and most of them feel that Allah hears their prayers. These Muslims simply want to be left alone, and they have no mind to rule the world, let alone rule you. Many of those Muslims live in the United States. If you ask them about what I have said they will tell you that I am full of it, and that theirs is a religion of peace. But deep down they know differently. In fact, their Koran speaks way more about violent Jihad than it does about peace.

Who really rules the roost when it comes to Islam? The answer to that is somewhat simple: whatever group can gain and maintain power over the people it seeks to rule. Whether it is a Mullah, Caliph, Imam, or a dictator, Islamic rulers are the ones who are able to declare what the Koran says, and what it means. The followers of these leaders range from the barely educated to the well educated. They are the supposed "true believers" in and of the Islamic way. This is so despite the different teachings these leaders profess. Ultimately, the only thing that really matters to all of these Muslims is the inevitability of a Muslim dominated and ruled world. Once that happens they will iron out their religious differences—which will be a bloody affair to behold when it happens.

What does all of this mean to you?

I don't care which brand of Islam you are dealing with (Sunni, Shiite, etc.) or where the followers of those brands are located in the world (including Saudi Arabia), they all believe in the inevitable: the religion of Islam and its true Muslim followers will one day rule the world.

This means that no matter what a true, practicing Muslim says about who he is, how he acts, or what he says he believes, his ultimate aim is to forward his religion's goal: ruling the world and making Muslims of everyone in it. How many different ways can I stress that fact!

It's time for you to come up with, "Well Christians want everyone in the world to become Christian, don't they?"

Sorry, it's not the same thing. Christians would like everyone in the world to believe in, and follow, Christ, but they try to promote this by their words and their Christian actions of love and forgiveness. But Muslims have no such scruples. Their way (if at all possible) is to force Islam upon every man, woman, and child in the world, whether they like it or not. Most Muslims will say this is not so, that it is not the Muslim way. But, their ways are often quite subtle. Maybe you should study that religion if you don't believe what I have told you. Find these things out for yourself.

Last, remember this: It is a tenant of militant Islam to destroy first all Jews, then all Christians, then every country on earth that is not Muslim and/or a follower of Islam. Right now that looks like an impossible feat to accomplish. But, someday, maybe even in your lifetime, it just might become a reality. Don't say you weren't warned.

By the way, in my opinion the very fact that many Muslims will hate what I have said, proves the truth of my words. Ask them to show you how I am wrong. It might be interesting to see what they say, and how they try to spin their answers.

Below are the two definitions of the word, Jihad. (Remember, the word means *to struggle*). I hope this will help you when you are discussing this subject with your family, friends, and/or your brilliant college professors.

Jihad—Greater Jihad and Lesser Jihad:

1) Greater Jihad: One's inner mental and moral struggle with life in terms of the will of Allah.

2) Lesser Jihad: Fighting and conquering the enemies of Allah. This includes:
A. Moving to foreign lands to evangelize and multiply.
B. Oral Jihad, having to do with apologetics (explaining and defending Islam to others).
C. Written Jihad—distributing books sympathetic to Islam which help to both raise money and to evangelize non Muslims.
D. Construction—the building of as many mosques as possible in foreign countries around the world to use as places of prayer, and as meeting places to strategize against the enemies of Islam.
E. Monetary support—building banks and businesses in foreign countries, and levying taxes (wherever practical) on non Muslims. (Look up the term, "Jizya.")

F.   Intelligence—collecting information on or about Jews and Christians in hopes of finding things that later can be used against them.

G.   Waging war against the enemies of Islam using any means necessary to win that war. This includes every violent act imaginable.

You now know that the word, "Jihad," has many meanings, so don't get confused when you hear that word. Simply look to see how it is applied in the situation you are dealing with.

A word of caution: If you look around your town you may see an unexplainable influx of Muslims opening business there. This certainly does not mean that these "newcomers" are bad people in any way, or that they mean harm to anyone. And, I'm not saying to get all paranoid about seeing them in your midst—as long as they are here legally. I am saying to watch and see whether (or how many times) they try to circumvent the laws of your cities by using their religious beliefs as a tool to accomplish their Jihadist goals. Read again what it says in "D" above.

Don't be paranoid. Just watch. Be nice. And know that not all Middle-Eastern people are Muslim, and those who are, are not all radical Muslims unworthy to be called your friend.

Rickey

My name is Rickey. I was five years old when this . . . thing . . . started. Kindergarten was okay, but first grade was more fun. One reason it was fun was because Kathie was in my class. Kathie was my best friend; I really liked her. The nice thing was . . . she liked me too. Kathie and I would bring each other desserts from home like cookies and brownies; you know, things our mothers made.

I have a baby sister. She was real cute when she was young, and she still is. I loved to pick her up and kiss her all over her face and arms. She'd laugh so hard when I did that. I did too. My mom and dad were real happy that my little sister and I got along so good.

Kathie brought me some grapes one day, green ones. I love green grapes. I kissed her on the side of her head for bringing me those grapes. The bad thing was my teacher saw me kiss her head. She got all upset. She took me out in the hall and said she didn't ever want to see me kiss my friend, Kathie, again. I wasn't sure why she was so mad, but I said I wouldn't do it again. The whole thing made me kind of scared. No one got mad when I kissed my baby sister on the head. I didn't tell my mom; I was afraid she would get mad at me too, although she never got mad when I kissed my little sister.

On Valentines' Day I made a card for Kathie, but she was sick that day, so she didn't come to school. When she came back a week later I gave her my card and a Snickers bar too. She was real happy. She surprised me when she handed me a card she had made for me. After I read the card, Kathie handed me a huge Hershey bar with nuts in it. I was so happy that I reached down for her hand and I kissed it two times!

I guess the teacher had been watching us. When she saw me kiss Kathie's hand she ran over to me and she screamed at me. "I saw you do that," she said. She grabbed my arm and pulled me down to the principal's office. She told the principal what I did and he called up my mother to come and get me. When my mother got there the principal told her that I was being suspended, and that I might not be able to come back to his school. When she asked him what I did, he told her that I sexually harassed my classmate, Kathie.

My mother didn't say much. She looked confused and upset. She and my father argued that night, but I don't think they were mad at me. I think they were mad at the school, or something.

When I came back to school after my suspension ended all of the kids began to tease me. They called me a molester. It made Kathie cry. For some reason she was afraid to talk to me after that. After two weeks my parents had me go to another school.

I guess what I did went into my school record because no matter what school I went to after that people seemed to know that I had sexually molested a girl. I changed schools once again just before entering the eighth grade. I didn't know it at first but Kathie was going to the same school; I'd see her every once in a while but we never talked to each other. That always made me sad.

In the middle of the ninth grade I got into a fight with some guy who called me a child molester. He hit me in the face real hard. The next week my parents transferred me to a different school. I hoped that I would have a better time at that new school. I played basketball there. I wasn't very good, but it was fun . . . until someone in the office read my file. Not long after that everyone in the school began to tease me. All I did was kiss Kathie's hand! Why was everyone so mean to me?

During the tenth grade I didn't even have one friend. Finally, these two guys began to talk to me. They were nice guys although they talked kind of funny, but I liked both of them. I invited them over to my house one time. After they left my mother said that she didn't like them too much. She said they acted strange. Not long after that they told me that they were going to "come out." They asked me if I had any "gay feelings." It sort of surprised me. I told them I'd have to think about it. When I later told them, "No," they stopped talking to me, but not before saying that they thought I was anti-gay.

Toward the end of the eleventh grade a group of guys asked me if I would like to join their gang. They seemed to be okay guys. I didn't have any friends so I said that I would go around with them. It made me feel good that someone cared enough about me to want me to hang out with them. We went to places like the show and our school's football and basketball games. It was sort of fun. After several weeks I discovered that all of them smoked marijuana. I tried it because I didn't want them to think I was lame. It made me sick but I didn't tell them about it. I often pretended that I was smoking it, but I wouldn't inhale.

They also drank a lot of booze. Their older brothers would buy it for us. The alcohol made me forget about what I had done, and I began to care less and less about all the people who had hated me throughout my life. The only ones who didn't hate me were the members of my gang.

One night we went to this party. The party wasn't in our town. I didn't even know what school the people having the party went to. There was this girl there who was really drunk. My friends and some other guys took her into one of the bedrooms in the house. They told me that they were going to gang-rape her. I didn't know what to do; I didn't want to do that to her. When they began to do things to her, I slowly backed out of the room. I made my way to the living room of the house and was about to go outside when these two cops stopped me. They told me to go back into the house.

Soon everyone was in the front part of the house, including my friends. It was then announced that the girl I had seen had been raped. Two other cops had found her in a bathtub. She had been beaten and was covered with blood. The cops covered her with a blanket and brought her into the living room; they asked her if she could identify the people who had raped her. She looked around the room and finally pointed at my two friends. Then she looked at me and started to cry. She said that I was also one of the ones who had raped her.

The three of us were taken to jail where we were interrogated in three different rooms. Finally, the other two interrogators came onto my room. They told me that my two friends admitted that they had been in the room where the girl was raped, but only briefly, and that they left when I began to rape her because, "They didn't go along with that sort of thing." Those were the words they used.

Despite my protests, I was put into a jail cell and my "friends" were released. I spent almost a week in jail. While I was in jail it was determined that my DNA was not found anywhere on that girl. I was not told whose DNA they did find on her. I was released, and the girl seemed not to want to press charges on any of the other suspects.

At the end of the summer I made ready to begin my senior year, but just before school began my parents and I were informed that I was "not eligible" to attend my senior year at that school. When we asked why the principal told us that "my long record of sexual offenses made my attendance there impossible."

It was then that I decided that my life was worthless, and that I had been a looser ever since first grade. I had reached my limit. There was simply no reason to go on living. I resolved to kill myself. I got a gun from one of my old gang member friends who told me that he owed me for not naming him for raping that drunk girl. I hid the gun under my bed. It is still there.

As I write this I want to tell whoever reads it that I hate the guy who gave me this gun, and I hate all of his friends. I have considered killing all of them, but ending my own horrible life is even more important than doing that. The only thing is I can't get up the nerve to kill myself. I've put that gun in my mouth a dozen times, but I can't pull the trigger.

I have only one alternative: I have to do something to make the police do it for me.

I hate my school, my town, and all the people in it. I hate myself, too. I'm glad that I'm going to do what I've decided to do.

I am going to my school tomorrow morning and I will shoot as many people as I can. That will force the police to kill me. It is the only way.

I'm sorry, Mom and Dad. None of this is your fault.

I wish I hadn't kissed Kathie's hand.

Rickey

Thirty W's

"Why, when we wonder what Willie Williams will wipe Whitney White's window with, will we wonder, Wendy?" went Wondering Walt Witcomb whose wife woefully wondered why Wondering Walt was wondering.

Look in the W's of your dictionary to see if you can make this sentence even longer, or a different "W" sentence longer than that. Bet you can. See if you can do this with other letters of the alphabet. Have your kids try it.

Just an Observation

I went to Disneyland not long ago. It was during the week just before Christmas. There were so many people there you couldn't even move. And it was on a Monday! And Christmas vacation hadn't even begun for most of little brats that were there! Okay, I'll try to be nice this one time—*for most of the darling little kids that were there.*

Anyway, what surprised me more than anything was the fact that the noise level wasn't as high as it should have been in light of the number of people that were there. While I was sitting at the Carnation place waiting for the fireworks to begin, it suddenly dawned on me. The reason it was not as noisy as one would expect was because practically every person I saw was on his or her stupid ass cell phone!

I looked around for a second then decided to try to count how many people I could see who *were not* on their cell phone. I would give it twenty seconds. Not counting babies, kids under four, and old people like me, I counted a total of seven people out of an estimated 100 people that passed by who were not on their cell phone!

I'll tell you what. I'm glad I only have a few years left to live on this planet because you younger people are headed for disaster, and I don't want to be here to see it! And don't ask me why. You already know the answer to that from my other rantings.

Two Poems

The following two poems are from an unpublished book of sixty poems that I wrote a number of years ago entitled, A CHILD'S MODERN GARDEN OF VERSES. From a writer's standpoint, a poetry book is very difficult to publish—unless one wants to self-publish his work. So, I simply wrote this book of children's poetry and filed it away without ever sending it to a publishing company. It seemed like a good way to end this book (RANTINGS OF AN OLD MAN) which is, of course, a title most of you think was/is quite appropriate.

Two poems from a book of poetry entitled, A CHILD'S MODERN GARDEN OF VERSES by Michael Blade (that's me):

"Johnny Casper"

Johnny Casper was an athlete who played professional ball;
He was the youngest, and the smartest, and the fastest of
them all.

The game was for the title, the score was eight to three;
Johnny's team was five behind, the price of one TD.

Twenty seconds now read the clock, just time for two more
plays—
"Red wing shuttle," said the quarterback; John smiled a far-
off gaze.

A dazzling fake, then he was off, bounding like a deer,
And in a flash, Johnny knew that he was in the clear.

The crowd then roared, his teammates cheered,
His opponents began to moan,

As Johnny Casper, leaped at last,
Into the striped end-zone.

The pigskin twirled high in the air, then began its fall;
John's grin was wide as he reached out—then Casper
dropped the ball!

The shock-filled crowd was still at first, then silence turned
to groans,
And Johnny felt a sickening chill, that shot straight though
his bones.

"Time out!" was called as John turned back, his head now in a muddle,
And then his ears began to burn as he approached the huddle.

Not one player said a word as John rejoined the pack,
And as he bent low, he sought the eyes, of the quarterback.

The "Q" then nodded as though he knew, and without another sound,
He looked at Casper, then said aloud, "Fifteen pitch-out, end-around."

The clock had nine more ticks to go, when the center hiked the ball,
Then came the pitch to Johnny C.; no way would he now fall.

John tucked the ball; he gnashed his teeth; he turned the end-around,
And as he ran, hot bodies flew, and crashed upon the ground.

The pack of wolves sought Johnny out, but John ran like a steer;
Then came the hole he knew he'd find, and John was in the clear.

The wolves soon fell, one by one, as Johnny pulled away,
And the screaming crowd went wild as he reached the goal that day.

The gun went off; Johnny's team had won; the proof was
in the score,
But, the fans all left in sadness, as they knew John would
play no more.

The years have passed and the crowd is still, but if you
bend an ear,
You'll hear a whisper in the wind, "Johnny Casper once
played here."

Michael Blade

"Watercolor-Blue"

My dad made me a glider
Out of paper and some glue,
And when it dried we painted it
With watercolor-blue.

On each wing we drew a star,
And on its tail we placed
A picture of a lightning bolt,
And then outside I raced.

There was no wind, but I didn't care,
I cocked my arm to see
Just how far my glider would go,
How fast my plane would be.

It turned a loop, then shot straight down,
Its flight was short, but smooth.
If only a strong wind would come,
Then my plane would move!

I made my way straight down the path
That ends up on the hill
That overlooks the great wide sea,
But no wind was there still.

I cocked my arm—way back this time—
And I threw with all my might,
And as I let go, a great wind arose,
I raised my fist, "All right!"

My glider shot into the sky,
Higher and higher it flew.
Oh! What a thrill it was to see
That streaking jet of blue.

The wind continued, stronger now,
Then it had been before.
Circles and loops my stunt plane did;
I could hear its engine roar.

The urge to follow it crossed my mind
As it headed toward the sea,
But the cliff I was on prevented it;
"Oh wind, bring it back to me!"

I stood there for the longest time,
'Till "Blue" had become a dot,
And I still return from time to time,
And I stand on that very same spot.

While there I think about my dad,
And the plane he made for me;
Watercolor-Blue that streaked the
sky, Then headed out to sea.

(P.S. I know it's voguish to use anything but rhyme when writing poetry. But, I like poetry that rhymes, especially for young people. If I stay alive long enough to write another book I'll include in its contents two of my poems that do not rhyme—just for those who like that sort of peotry.)

One more thing before we say good-bye: It may be interesting for you to know that in 2011 I sold almost everything I owned and gave nearly all of my wealth to a series of charities that needed the money far more than I did (or do). My children agreed beforehand that they needed none of those funds as they are all well off. I now live in a rented mobile home near the west coast and am able to pay my bills with the aid of a small 401K that I did not give away, and an equally small monthly Social Security check. This may not be how you might have envisioned my life to be at this point, but it is the way I want it to be. What's more, it is the way I intend it to remain until I am no more.

And now it's time to say, "Farewell."

I'll leave you with these two statements. The first statement is my own thought. I'm sorry to say that I don't know who wrote the second statement as there are a number of claims in terms of its authorship.

1. Truth has nothing to do with how many people believe it.

2. Yesterday is history. Tomorrow is a mystery. Today is a gift. That's why it's called the present.

Farewell,

MB

THE END